Praise for *Abolishing Abortion*

We in public office cannot do our job unless the church does her job. In *Abolishing Abortion*, Father Pavone gives a stirring call to both church and state to protect the unborn. This book is a must for all who want to heed that call!

—Governor Sam Brownback of Kansas

Father Pavone insightfully writes that *Roe v. Wade* didn't just subvert the principle that no government can authorize the killing of the innocent, it subverted the very government our nation's Founders created. *Abolishing Abortion* is about saving lives, but it's also about saving our republic.

—Mike Huckabee, former Governor of Arkansas,
former host of *Huckabee*, on the Fox News Channel

I have known no better warrior in the fight to protect every human life than Father Pavone. His new book *Abolishing Abortion* makes the compelling case that the pro-life cause defends the same principles for which our Founding Fathers fought. As they pledged their lives, fortunes, and sacred honor, so must we!

—Senator Rick Santorum, former US Senator, Pennsylvania

A practical roadmap for those of us who share [Fr. Pavone's] commitment to defending life in the womb.

—Jim Daly, president, Focus on the Family

Just as my uncle, Rev. Martin Luther King, Jr., fanned the flames of the civil rights movement, so today Rev. Frank Pavone is doing the same for the movement to end abortion.

—Dr. Alveda King, niece of Martin Luther King,
Jr., commentator on Fox News Channel

Father Frank Pavone has written an eloquent, timely, and eminently practical account of how to take advantage of the horror abortion inspires in order to put an end to it.

—Russell Shaw, former Secretary for Public
Affairs of the US Bishops' Conference

Father Pavone has written a powerful book, one that makes the case that 55 million abortions in America since 1973 defies the principle that the sanctity and dignity of each and every life is precious in the eyes of Providence.

—TIM GOEGLEIN, VICE PRESIDENT, FOCUS ON THE FAMILY

Abolishing Abortion is [Fr. Pavone's] road map to put an end to the holocaust of abortion. What could be more important than heeding his advice?

—BRENT BOZELL, FOUNDER AND PRESIDENT,
MEDIA RESEARCH CENTER

In *Abolishing Abortion*, Fr. Frank has provided for us a solid blueprint and the knowledge pro-lifers of every denomination, age, and ethnicity need to restore the right to life of the unborn.

—ASTRID BENNETT GUTIERREZ, PRESIDENT, HISPANICS FOR LIFE

This book helps every pro-lifer to connect his or her pro-life convictions to the actions that government officials and other leaders need to take in order to end abortion in America.

—REV. TERRY GENSEMER, DIRECTOR, CEC FOR
LIFE (CHARISMATIC EPISCOPAL CHURCH)

In *Abolishing Abortion*, [Fr. Pavone] presents a clear and compelling case for why abortion will become unthinkable and unavailable in our lifetimes . . . if we take the strong, purposeful steps he recommends.

—BRIAN FISHER, COFOUNDER AND PRESIDENT, ONLINE FOR LIFE

Fr. Frank is one of the few priests I know whose only mission is to save the blessed God-given life that comes from our Creator. No exceptions, no excuses.

—DENISE F. COCCIOLONE, FOUNDER AND
PRESIDENT, NATIONAL LIFE CENTER

Abolishing Abortion is an excellent new resource for those interested in the connection between faith and living that faith in the public square.

—MARJORIE DANNENFELSER, PRESIDENT, SUSAN B. ANTHONY LIST

Abolishing Abortion is an important book to encourage and guide all of us to join in combating the greatest evil of our times.

—Phyllis Schlafly, chairman, Eagle Forum

Even for those of us who have been leaders in the movement for many years, Fr. Frank Pavone always brings fresh and challenging insights into the problem of abortion and new inspiration to work to end it.

—Peggy Hartshorn, president, Heartbeat International

Father Frank Pavone has written a compelling and eloquent book about the importance of protecting human life.

—Gary Bauer, president, American Values

When you read *Abolishing Abortion*, you will come away not only saying, "No more excuses," but, "What can I do to make a difference?"

—Teresa Tomeo, media expert, motivational speaker, bestselling author, syndicated Catholic talk show host of *Catholic Connection* and *The Catholic View for Women*

This book is a beam of light that pierces the fog of the abortion industry, and those who aid and abet them.

—Troy Newman, director, Operation Rescue

ABOLISHING ABORTION

ABOLISHING ABORTION

How You Can Play a Part in Ending
the Greatest Evil of Our Day

Rev. Frank Pavone

NELSON
BOOKS

An Imprint of Thomas Nelson

Published in Nashville, Tennessee, by Nelson Books, an imprint of Thomas Nelson. Nelson Books and Thomas Nelson are registered trademarks of HarperCollins Christian Publishing, Inc.

Author is represented by the literary agency of Global Lion Intellectual Property Management, Inc., P.O. Box 669238, Pompano Beach, Florida 33066.

Interior designed by James Phinney.

Thomas Nelson, Inc., titles may be purchased in bulk for educational, business, fund-raising, or sales promotional use. For information, please e-mail SpecialMarkets@ThomasNelson.com.

Unless otherwise indicated, Scripture quotations are from the REVISED STANDARD VERSION of the Bible. © 1946, 1952, 1971, 1973 by the Division of Christian Education of the National Council of the Churches of Christ in the U.S.A. Used by permission.

Scripture quotations marked ESV are taken from THE ENGLISH STANDARD VERSION. © 2001 by Crossway Bibles, a division of Good News Publishers.

Scripture quotations marked KJV are taken from the Holy Bible, King James Version (public domain).

Scripture quotations marked NASB are taken from the NEW AMERICAN STANDARD BIBLE®, © The Lockman Foundation 1960, 1962, 1963, 1968, 1971, 1972, 1973, 1975, 1977, 1995. Used by permission.

Scripture quotations marked NIV are taken from the New International Version˚, NIV˚. Copyright © 1973, 1978, 1984, 2011 by Biblica, Inc.™ Used by permission of Zondervan. All rights reserved worldwide. www.zondervan.com.

Library of Congress Cataloging-in-Publication Data

Pavone, Frank A.
Abolishing abortion : how you can play a part in ending the greatest evil of our day / Fr. Frank Pavone.
pages cm
Includes bibliographical references.
ISBN 978-1-4002-0572-1
1. Abortion--Religious aspects--Catholic Church. 2. Abortion--United States. 3. Pro-life movement--United States. I. Title.
HQ767.3.P39 2015
362.1988'80973--dc23

2014038437

Printed in the United States of America

15 16 17 18 19 RRD 6 5 4 3 2 1

I dedicate this book to my youngest brothers and sisters, the children still in the womb, and to all those who, in ways big and small, sacrifice themselves to save them.

CONTENTS

CONTENTS

INTRODUCTION

Us and Them

AMONG THE GREAT MEN AND WOMEN I HAVE BEEN PRIVILEGED to know, none stands taller than the physically diminutive Mother Teresa. I remember visiting with her in Calcutta just a few months after she gave her well-known speech at the National Prayer Breakfast in Washington, DC, in 1994.

Speaking boldly that day in the presence of President and Mrs. Clinton, both of them beholden to the abortion industry, Mother Teresa ignored all the taboos about raising controversial subjects in a public forum. Well into her talk, she startled those gathered by saying, "I feel that the greatest destroyer of peace today is abortion, because it is a war against the child, a direct killing of the innocent child, murder by the mother herself. And if we accept that a mother can kill even her own child, how can we tell other people not to kill one another?"[1]

Her argument was so powerful there could be no rebuttal.

The opposition tries to keep those who are pro-life out of the public square precisely for this reason: they know that if they let us in, they lose.

"Many of the American people loved your speech," I told her at the time.

"And what about the rest of them?" she responded.

It's a good question. What about the rest of them? And are "we" all not sometimes "them"? None of us, me included, has done enough to end the nightmare of abortion, but end it we can. I have written this book to show how.

A BONE IN THE THROAT

Our project of abolishing abortion is a long, hard struggle. Abortion is like the bone stuck in the throat of the American people. We can't swallow it, and yet we can't quite get rid of it either. It plagues us. It poisons us. And yet, we seem eternally stuck with it.

Public opinion, conflicted as it is, has moved very little over the decades. Americans love life, and they love freedom too. In abortion, these priorities seem to collide, and as a nation, we don't quite know how to manage the collision. When we try to raise the issue and press for a resolution, we find obstacles at every turn:

- When we speak about abortion in church, we're told it's too political.
- When we speak about it in the political arena, we're told it's too religious.
- When we try to raise the issue in the media, we're told it is too disturbing.
- When we dare speak of it in the world of business, we are told it is too distracting.
- When we try to introduce it in a classroom, we are told it's too controversial.
- When we take our message to the streets, we are told it is too disruptive.

So if abortion is wrong, where do we go to say so? We go where the opposition does not want us to: into the churches, into politics, into the media, into the business world, into education, and into the streets! This has been, and continues to be, my journey. Traveling some 80 percent of the time, often to as many as four states a week, I find myself looking forward to each day as if it were the first day of my mission.

When I was just beginning this mission, I had to smile when a friend told me that he was happy I was "finally able to do my thing." It is not "my thing," I reminded him gently. It is everyone's thing, everyone's responsibility, because unless the unborn are safe, none of us are safe.

Although I write from a Catholic perspective, and many of my struggles have been within the Catholic hierarchy, human nature is much the same wherever we encounter it. Our allies in this movement—Christian, Jewish, Muslim, and secular—will have endured many comparable struggles and will, I hope, learn from my experience. Then too, as Americans, we all participate in the struggle against a state that is cold and indifferent, if not downright hostile. My experience in confronting the state is equally relevant to people of all traditions.

Before we can win over the state, however, we must first win over our churches, temples, and mosques. We cannot rest until we do. Our mission is to reach the rest of them until there are no more of "them" to be reached—and remember that "them" begins with "us."

ONE

In the Public Square

IN JANUARY 2014, THE NOMINALLY CATHOLIC GOVERNOR OF New York, Andrew Cuomo, publicly declared that people "who are right-to-life" were among those who "have no place in the state of New York, because that's not who New Yorkers are."[1] Cuomo merely said out loud what others of his mind-set say among themselves.

He was, of course, wrong on many different levels—morally, civically, and prophetically. Not only do pro-lifers belong in the public square but we will also one day own it. To accomplish this, we must first know why we belong and then understand what we need to do to prevail.

ACCEPTING THE PRICE

The fifty-six men who signed the Declaration of Independence did not do so lightly. When they signed, "with a firm reliance on the protection of divine Providence" and "pledge[d] to each other our Lives, our Fortunes and our sacred Honor," they did so knowing their signatures could cost them their lives and their fortunes. As to "sacred honor," that could not be taken away, but under duress, it could be surrendered.

First among the "unalienable rights" the signers pledged to protect was "life." Legalized abortion clearly violates the principles they risked all for. It is not simply a "bad policy" or an "unjust law," but rather, it marks the dissolution of this nation's most fundamental contract with its citizens. The battle against abortion demands—no less than the founding of this country demanded—a steely resolve and a willingness to accept the price of engagement. I make a plea in these pages that we accept these risks. If need be, we have to be prepared to lay down our lives for our unborn brothers and sisters.

We cannot escape risk in this battle. Nor can we fit the battle into our lifestyle. We must fit our lifestyle into the battle and interrupt our patterns of convenience and comfort as need be. The champions of abortion do not rest. Neither can we. The battle to defend the children in the womb—that one segment of humanity whose rights are most cruelly denied—is a battle for humanity itself. And it is worth everything.

There are certain battles in life and in history that call for the commitment of every fiber of one's being, every ounce of one's life and strength, for the whole of life. Ending abortion is one of them. That's the power of this cause. And that's the essence of this book: a call to cast off the shackles by which we limit ourselves, because those indeed are the most powerful shackles of all. We are responsible for breaking out of our denial, our fear, and our unwillingness to sacrifice for the cause of life.

I remember the day early in my priesthood when the iron door closed behind me. I knew then I had to devote my life to this battle. It is a battle that, once commenced, can never be abandoned. I judge no one else's commitment, and I respect the limits that others face. In the final analysis, victory will not require vast multitudes of people, but rather relatively small numbers willing to take immense risks. I am hoping the readers of this book will be among them. For me, compromise and moderation are not options. I am reminded of the stirring words of abolitionist William Lloyd Garrison when asked to moderate his stand against slavery:

> I am aware that many object to the severity of my language; but is there not cause for severity? I will be as harsh as truth, and as uncompromising as justice. On this subject, I do not wish to think,

or to speak, or write, with moderation. No! No! Tell a man whose house is on fire to give a moderate alarm; tell him to moderately rescue his wife from the hands of the ravisher; tell the mother to gradually extricate her babe from the fire into which it has fallen— but urge me not to use moderation in a cause like the present. I am in earnest—I will not equivocate—I will not excuse—I will not retreat a single inch—AND I WILL BE HEARD. The apathy of the people is enough to make every statue leap from its pedestal, and to hasten the resurrection of the dead.[2]

Our language need not be severe. Our goal, after all, is to make converts, not enemies, but we must be prepared to call things by their names and do what Saint Paul said we must do regarding the works of darkness: "Expose them!" (Eph. 5:11). To accomplish this, we would do well to emulate Garrison's tenacity. Like Garrison in his crusade against slavery, we must not equivocate. We must not retreat a single inch. We must be heard!

OWN THE PUBLIC SQUARE

Soon after a major election in which many pro-life candidates had won, I received several encouraging e-mails about the homily I had given on Eternal Word Television Network (EWTN) just before Election Day. "I never in my life put so much effort into and felt so good about my vote," wrote one correspondent who took it upon herself to research all the relevant candidates and share what she learned. "I will in the future remember what I heard this morning and always research my candidates and not just vote in haste. Wouldn't it be great if everyone went through that effort, maybe things would change for the better?"

Soon after, I heard from a correspondent who was inspired to do something he rarely did—vote! To do this meant fixing a flat on a rainy day even before going to work. "I felt a strong compulsion to go and make my voice and vote count for all the pre-born babies that will never get the chance to vote," he wrote. "I knew that I was responding to God's call to do my part. I was so energized when leaving the polling station I forgot completely about all the obstacles impeding me casting my vote."

When I begin to respond to so many of the misconceptions about "separation of church and state," I think of these e-mails. They exemplify how church and state are supposed to work together. The Church—and by "the Church" I mean the spectrum of Christian churches, the entire Body of Christ—does not set up the voting booths, but it motivates and equips people to go into them and make a difference. The Church does not write the laws, but bears witness to the truth of God to which those laws must correspond. Politics is not our salvation; Jesus Christ is. But fidelity to Him includes doing our part as faithful citizens, and to exercise our rights as citizens appropriately, we have to understand the relationship between the Church and the state, and how both of these entities are responsible for protecting and safeguarding the right to life.

After Jesus rose from the dead, He said, "All authority in heaven and on earth has been given to me. Go therefore and make disciples of all nations, baptizing them in the name of the Father and of the Son and of the Holy Spirit, teaching them to observe all that I have commanded you. And behold, I am with you always, to the end of the age" (Matt. 28:18–20 ESV). Having been given "all the authority in heaven and on earth," those disciples who saw Jesus after His resurrection would confirm, as Mark reported, "The kingdom of God has come with power" (Mark 9:1). To understand the mission of the Church, and her relationship with the state and with politics, we must first understand the person of Jesus Christ, who rules the universe with all authority, all power, and all dominion.

To prevail in the public square, we must take the Incarnation seriously. Jesus is *really* God and Man. If we look at the different heresies in regard to who Jesus is, we find the source of the misunderstanding about the nature of the Church and its relationship to the world, to the state, and to politics. For example, there is the old heresy that says Jesus only appeared to be human. He didn't really exist as a human being. He didn't really suffer. He didn't really die. This gave rise to a form of Christianity that is actually overspiritualized, and an overspiritualized Church can easily end up being overly disengaged from the world.

Then there's the other extreme, that Jesus Christ was a man and nothing other. Although specially appointed by God, He was still a man, who did not really share the divine nature. If that's the starting point for an understanding of Jesus Christ, it reduces the Church to just another human institution, like the state, one whose power is only political, only human, and whose goal is an earthly paradise. If we see the Church as only spiritual or only human, we lose sight of its distinct identity and its distinct contribution to the political arena. In reality, Christ and therefore the Church are both human and divine. The Church encompasses *everything* that's human. The Church takes humanity seriously. For the Church, "matter" matters.

In a similar vein, the problems that we face today regarding the sanctity of life, marriage, and sexuality reflect a mistaken view of the human person. When people say, "My body, my choice" or "I can do what I want with my body," what do they really mean? Is your body a thing that you do something with, or is it *you*? The Church has always proclaimed that the body is an aspect of the person. So the body is not a mere object that you do something with, like, say, a hammer or a car. Your body is *you*. As soon as you say, "I can do what I want with my body," you create a separation between yourself and your body. You're over here and your body is over there, and you're doing something with it. So often, in fact, we hear people who have done something they know to be wrong, even criminal, speak as though they were somehow removed from the person committing the wrong.

This is not the Church's view of the human person. The Church encompasses everything that is human and takes matter so seriously that the physical body *is* the person just as much as the spiritual soul is. In other words, the Church proclaims a living unity of body and soul. The Church exists precisely because the Kingdom of God has broken into the world. Both its origin and its destiny are from above. We're not seeking to build up some kind of earthly paradise, but neither can we forget that we are, indeed, living on earth today.

So what is the relationship between the Kingdom and the world? After Jesus said, "All authority . . . has been given to me," He told the apostles—and us by extension—to go and change the world.

WAITING ACTIVELY

"Go therefore and make disciples of all the nations," said Jesus (Matt. 28:19 NASB). All humanity, every human being ever created, is called to follow Christ and to share the benefits of the new and everlasting covenant. The Church has a commission: to make disciples of all the nations, to carry out everything Jesus has commanded. No one is exempt.

The same people who belong to the Church also belong to the state. Because one and the same person belongs to both, there is a necessary connection. The connection is rooted in us as individuals, and in our actions. And when we begin to ask whether our actions are good or bad, right or wrong, we enter the arena of morality. When the state looks at our actions, it's concerned about right or wrong in terms of the law. When the Church looks at our actions, it is concerned about right or wrong in terms of our relationship with God and our eternal salvation. We have been called to be part of the

Kingdom of God, and yet at the same time we have to organize ourselves politically in our society.

The Second Vatican Council's *Pastoral Constitution on the Church in the Modern World* is one of the richest documents ever issued, especially on the subject of the relationship between church and state, and it's useful to Christians of all stripes. The document acknowledges that the Kingdom of God has broken into the world, and therefore the Church exists. The state exists as well, as we are reminded every April 15, if not more often. How, then, does the growth of the Kingdom relate to human activity and the growth of nations and states?

The analysis contained in the document is marvelous. It argues that the progress of humankind is not to be confused with the growth of the Kingdom of God. They are distinct. We are not, however, to see Church and state as totally separate. All of the good that God's grace enables us to accomplish in this life—the acts of justice, of brotherhood, of peace—is not lost in the Kingdom of God. God does not overlook the good that we are able to do as individuals, as groups, and as nations. Rather, God uses these good efforts as building blocks of the Kingdom. The good things we produce in this world will endure in the world to come.

The document reminds us, however, that the Kingdom is brought to its fulfillment only by the Second Coming of Christ. We do not look for an earthly paradise. We do not look for a utopia. We look for Christ to come again. But while looking for Him to come again, we do not wait passively. *We wait actively.* To be sure, every good that we do in this world is compromised by evil and error and is somehow even deformed and tainted by sin. Yet we move forward in bringing about as much good as we can because we know that when He comes again, He is going to take the good we have been able to bring about in this world and purify it. He is going to lift it up.

ACTING JUDICIOUSLY

As we wait actively, we must also remind ourselves to act judiciously. Passion does not preclude good judgment and a measure of reserve. The Church, starting with Jesus Himself, has looked at the state with reservation, saying both yes and no. Importantly, the Christian "no" to the state is based on the very nature of Christianity as a "kingdom . . . not of this world," the phrase Jesus used when Pilate asked Him whether or not He was a king (John 18:33–36 NIV).

When the spies of the chief priests asked Jesus about paying tax to the emperor, He asked whose image was on the coin and was told "Caesar's." Said Jesus, "Then give back to Caesar what is Caesar's, and to God what is God's" (Luke 20:24–25 NIV). Implied in what Jesus said is, that which bears the image of God—namely, human beings, including Caesar himself—belongs to God. So here Christ established the framework: Caesar himself belongs to God. The state itself belongs to God. Caesar must obey God!

The Church has always held that the state does not contain the fullness of human hope or embrace the totality of human existence. Nor can we allow the state to claim our absolute loyalty and obedience. The state exists for the human person, not the other way around. Our destiny ultimately is not the here and now, but the new heavens and the new earth. So we can never put our ultimate hope and trust in what the state can do for us. This is the Church's "no" to the state. This understanding frees us from the myth of political salvation. The Church does not ask us to put ultimate hope and trust in any political party, candidate, or system. We can and should enter the public square, but it does not hold our destiny.

At the same time, the Church says a profound "yes" to the state. This affirmation is rooted in the simple reality that all authority, all power, comes from God. The fact that there is an earthly, civil authority that we need to obey becomes part of our obedience to God. Scripture is filled with examples of this. Even when the state and the powers of civil authority persecute believers, believers are exhorted to be good citizens.

Chapter 29 of the book of the prophet Jeremiah talks about the people being taken into exile in Babylon. They are not told to rebel. They are not asked to overthrow the Babylonian authorities. What they are called to do is "build houses and live in them; plant gardens and eat their produce. Take wives and have sons and daughters; take wives for your sons that they may bear sons and daughters; multiply there, and do not decrease. But seek the welfare of the city where I have sent you into exile, and pray to the LORD on its behalf, for in its welfare you will find your welfare" (Jer. 29:4–7). In other words, we are to seek the welfare of the state, even if the state treats us unjustly.

In the New Testament, Peter said, "Maintain good contact among the Gentiles, so that in case they speak against you as wrong-doers they may see your good deeds and glorify God. . . . Honor all men, love the brotherhood, fear God, honor the emperor. . . . Let none of you suffer as a murderer, or a thief, or a wrongdoer . . . yet if one suffers as a Christian, let him not be ashamed" (1 Peter 2:12, 17; 4:15–16). There are several other examples as well, including the exhortation to pay taxes and Jesus Himself paying the temple tax. Saint Augustine has a beautiful passage on the Church's "yes" to the state. In *The City of God* he wrote:

We all know how often the Body of Christ, his Church, is perse-cuted by the rulers of this world, but in what way do Christians injure the worldly state? I ask again, in what way do Christians injure the worldly state? Perhaps Christ their eternal King has for-bidden soldiers to enroll in the service of worldly authority? Did not he himself say when the Jews attempted to trap him, "Give to Caesar what is Caesar's and to God what is God's"? Did he not pay taxes with a coin taken from the fish's mouth? Did not one of his followers, a close companion on his journey, say to his colleagues, to Christ's fellow citizens, "Let everyone submit to civil authority" and order the Church to pray for the emperor? In what way then are Christians the State's enemies? In what way are Christians not subject to the kings who rule this earth?"[3]

To put it simply, the fact that we are citizens of heaven does not give us the right to ignore our duties as citizens of earth. One of the old criticisms of religion is that because we focus on a world to come, we are less concerned about this one. But the Church's teaching has always been very clear. Our preparation for the world to come makes us, if anything, more concerned about this one. It is a new heaven and a new earth that God is preparing for us, but one that has a very real connection to the way we have ordered ourselves in this un-heavenly world.

YOUR ROLE AS RULER

In 1 Samuel 8, the people of God were living on the land amid other nations with strange gods and strange rituals. But there was one major political difference between God's people and the other nations. They had kings. The people of Israel, focused as they were on the Lord, the covenant, and the commandments God gave to Moses, had not yet elevated a king from their ranks. So one day they asked the prophet Samuel why they alone did not have a king. They complained that all the other nations had rulers leading them into battle and providing for their needs, but they did not. Samuel responded that the Lord was their King. At the time, however, that response did not suffice. The Israelites wanted an earthly king.

So Samuel went to the Lord, and the Lord said, "They asked you for a king, give them a king. But warn them that they're going to suffer for it." Several chapters later we read the instructions that Samuel gave to the people: "Behold, the Lord has set a king over you. If you will fear the LORD and serve him and hearken to his voice and not rebel against the commandment of the LORD, and if both you and the king who reigns over you will follow the LORD your God, it will be well." That much said, Samuel offered a caveat: "But if you will not hearken to the voice of the LORD and rebel against the commandment of the LORD, then the hand of the LORD will be against you and your king" (1 Sam. 12:14–15). The hierarchy had been established, but it was based on a very specific understanding. The subject obeys the king, but the subject and the king obey the Lord.

In reading the Old Testament, we actually learn the history of two interwoven kingdoms: Israel, the Northern Kingdom of the ten tribes, and Judah. This is not, however, just history. It is theological history. It is history as seen from the perspective of God. If we analyze the many battles the people of Israel and Judah had with the surrounding nations from a political or military perspective, we might say, "They didn't seize the high ground," or "They didn't have a sufficient number of soldiers," or "They didn't place their army properly." In fact, we can find examples both of brilliance and blundering incompetence when we assess these battles tactically. Scripture, however, is a spiritual guide, not a tactical one. What the Scripture tells us is that when the people *and* their king observed the covenant and obeyed it, God preserved them from their enemies. But when they ignored that covenant, often at the urging of a sinful king, God Himself delivered them into their enemies' hands.

At the time of the Babylonian exile, the prophet Jeremiah was preaching the Word of God, but the people saw him as a traitor and threw him into a cistern. They were angry because Jeremiah was telling the people to submit to the Babylonians when they were itching to resist. He explained that resistance was futile because the Lord Himself had allowed their captivity as punishment for their sins, and that they would be permitted to return at the time of His choosing, not theirs, but this was not a message they wanted to hear.

In the Old Testament we read about evil kings who strayed so far as to sacrifice their sons and daughters to false gods and goddesses. Scripture tells us that this is ultimately why both the Babylonian exile and the Assyrian exile, the one that wiped out the ten northern tribes, were allowed to happen. It was the kings who were building the false altars, not the people. Responsibility rested on the shoulders of the sovereigns, but the people followed after them, and God punished both kings and people alike.

The message should be clear for all of us. Although God allowed for the creation of kingdoms, He held that both king and subjects had to honor the covenant, and ultimately subjects were held to account if either they or their king failed to do so. Today in America we bear even more responsibility than the prophets who spoke to the kings. We too are prophets by our baptism into Christ. We have a prophetic role, not in the sense of telling the future but of speaking the Word of God in the present. We do it as clergy when we preach, but we all do so as laypeople when we bear witness to the Word of God in our daily lives.

Like the prophets, we can speak to our "kings," those with political authority. Unlike the prophets, we can choose our kings. This is what gives us more responsibility than the people in the Old Testament ever had, and even more than the prophets. If our system of governance works the way it is designed to work, we, in fact, govern ourselves. What this means is that we bear the responsibility of a king. All the scriptural responsibilities that God places on the ruler are placed on us.

As we read the Bible from beginning to end, we see the burden placed on the ruler's shoulders. The ruler was to execute justice, reaffirm the covenant, lead the people in the ways of the Lord, promote peace, defend life, feed the poor, and protect the widowed. In choosing our own leaders, we become leaders ourselves. As Christians in America, we share the sovereign's burden. We cannot abandon the public square with any better conscience than a king could.

REAFFIRMING THE COVENANT

Each of us being a ruler in America, we have no need to establish a theocracy. In fact, we do not want a state in which, by law, people have to believe in the divinity of Christ or face fines if they fail to attend church on Sunday. We don't need to establish a theocracy because the truth has a power of its own, and we, as rulers, have the power to embrace it. The state can only interfere with this order.

The question remains, though, how does the truth reach the people? And the answer is by being proclaimed. I believe; therefore, I speak. The Word is preached and the seed is sown. The dignity of the human person requires that he or she hears it and accepts it freely. Jesus didn't force His message. He preached the Word, and the living power of the truth itself found its way into the human heart and mind—then as now. How did God create us? By speaking. "In the beginning was the Word" (John 1:1). We are made according to the truth, and therefore, when we hear the word of truth, it resonates.

The Church stands for religious liberty. Some have misinterpreted liberty to mean religious indifferentism, but there's a crucial difference. Religious indifferentism says we cannot require people to belong to any particular religion because all religions are the same and are of equal value. In this understanding, people choose whatever religion they want and then pick the teachings from that religion that suit their tastes, smorgasbord-style. Many people think this is what freedom of religion means.

But the Church does not think that way. The Church does not defend religious liberty based on the idea that all religions are equal. The Church defends religious liberty based on the idea that all people are equal. We are all icons of God. The divinely instilled dignity that we all share requires each of us to embrace the truth freely, without coercion—just as God acts without coercion in perfect freedom.

This does not mean there is no such thing as "truth." There is, to be sure, much confusion on this subject. Some believe that freedom to choose means that all choices are equally valid. The Church says it matters very much which one we choose. There is only one path to salvation, Jesus Christ. And Jesus Christ has laid out some very clear teachings that have been preserved and handed down to the apostles and taught to this very day. They're not taught because they're consoling, but because they're *true*.

It is, again, the dignity of the human person that requires us to embrace these truths freely. We're not talking about passing laws or electing candidates who are going to enact the covenant by requiring us to celebrate certain observances or lead certain prayers. But just as in the Old Testament, the leaders, the rulers, must reaffirm the covenant. And in America, we are the rulers.

UNIVERSAL RIGHTS

Let's put another piece of the puzzle in place. Yes, the Church teaches religious truths and revealed dogmas, but the Church also teaches truths that we can know by human reason alone. These are natural truths and fundamental rights we could discern even without the Church.

The difference between religious truths and natural truths is fairly clear. The Church, for instance, teaches the mystery of the Holy Trinity, a truth we could not come to by human reason alone. God shares one essence among three Persons. They are coequal. There are relationships among the three, but we could not come to an understanding of that by human reason alone. That is a revealed dogma of faith.

The Church also teaches, "Thou shalt not steal" (Ex. 20:15 KJV). To secure order in a functioning society, there must be a fundamental human right to property that cannot be breached without due process. This is an insight at which many people have arrived without being believers. Although it can be reached by human reason, the Church reinforces this truth. Still, we never hear people complain that the laws against theft represent an imposition of religious beliefs. And yet if we go to the Bible, we can hear this sanction on the lips of Jesus or on the tablets of Moses, which are inscribed by the finger of God. The Church reaffirms this truth because our fallen human nature inclines us to actions we know to be wrong. Still, we don't hear anyone say, "In America, I don't even have to be Christian. Therefore, I can steal." Instinctively, we all know better.

There is a third element in the formulation "church and state." The element common to both is morality. It is critical to understand "church, state, and morality" as one dynamic. We cannot just talk about church and state as separate entities with separate guidelines. There is a morality that flows through both. The sanctions on stealing or killing illustrate the shared norms. We affirm that the Church and the state each has a legitimate autonomy. Yet when we say that there is a legitimate separation of the two, willed by God Himself, we are not saying that the way we conduct ourselves politically is value-free. Democracy cannot be value-neutral. It cannot fail to ascertain that there are certain things that are good, certain things that are right. And yes, we can know those things.

Human reason is something that is shared by all of us. We don't all exercise it with the same degree of discernment, but a common denominator of humanity is our ability to reason. We are able to distinguish between right and wrong. We also understand that on certain issues right and wrong are so clearly distinct that the state absolutely must acknowledge them. We can discern, furthermore, the fundamental rights that people possess. A *fundamental right* is a human right without which we cannot express our humanity. At the top of the list are life itself and liberty. We cannot live as fully functioning persons if we are enslaved. A *person*, by definition, by his or her very nature, is free. We have to be able to act freely to accept our responsibility as humans. In America today and in all of the free world, this truth is fully accepted.

And yet to be free, a person must first be alive. To deprive a person of life is to deprive that person of liberty. It stands to reason, literally, that the very right to life has to be respected and protected. Life is an even more fundamental right than freedom. The Declaration of Independence confirmed the same—"life, liberty, and the pursuit of happiness," in that order. The state reinforces what the Church teaches. To hold the state accountable for protecting those fundamental rights has nothing to do with imposing religious beliefs and everything to do with reason.

THE LIMITS OF FREEDOM

While we are free to believe whatever we want, there are limits to how far we can go in acting on those beliefs. We might believe, for instance, that property is ill distributed, and it is our right to redistribute our neighbor's property by, say, stealing his car. We can believe that all we want, but the state believes otherwise and will promptly punish us if we put our thoughts into action. We are entitled to believe as well that our neighbor does not have a soul, but we are not permitted to enforce that belief by taking his life. The state protects his life despite what we believe.

The United States Supreme Court and lower courts have made this distinction in various religious freedom cases. Courts in Alabama and Tennessee, for example, ruled against churches that employed poisonous snakes in their ceremonies. With all due recognition of religious freedom, the courts argued that poisonous snakes endangered the lives and health of the believers. Note that the handling of the snakes in these cases was an integral part of the worship of those religious bodies.

In *Harden v. State*, a 1949 case out of Tennessee, the court ruled that congregants had the right to believe in snake handling "without fear of any punishment," but that their right to practice that belief was "limited by other recognized powers, equally precious to mankind." One of those precious rights was "that of society's protection from a practice, religious or otherwise, which is dangerous to life and health."[4]

In *Hill v. State*, a 1956 Alabama case, the court argued that the Constitution was not designed to exclude every act said to be religious from the legislative powers of the state. "Such a doctrine would lead to the constrained toleration of crime, equally abhorrent to the Jew and the Christian," ruled the court. Although the court affirmed that genuine religious acts should be immune from legislative prohibition, that immunity did not extend to acts "prejudicial to the public welfare, and productive of social injury."[5]

These decisions affirmed what the U.S. Supreme Court had ruled in the 1878 case *Reynolds v. U.S.*: "Suppose one believed that human sacrifices were a necessary part of religious worship. Would it be seriously contended that the civil government under which he lived could not prevent a sacrifice?"[6]

You must be wondering what snake handling and human sacrifice have to do with abortion. The point is simple. In each of these cases, the court has affirmed the individual's right to life. If it is not a violation of the "separation of church and state" for the state to tell a church not to kill innocent people, then neither is it a violation of the "separation of church and state" for a church to remind the state of its avowed obligation to protect innocent life. Both the church and the state have duties toward human life.

Ironically, abortionists and others who support the procedure often do so on the grounds of "religious freedom." They do so either explicitly or by invoking their spiritual convictions even while conceding that the act kills a child. Among the most memorable conversations I have had are with practicing abortionists. A number of them have admitted to me that they know they are killing a child, but they justify it by saying, "I don't know when the child receives a soul." I was stunned upon first hearing this and replied, "If you don't know when the child receives a soul, then you don't know whether the newborn has a soul. Does that then give you the right to kill the newborn?"

People are free to believe that the born or the unborn do or do not have souls, but the courts have ruled consistently that we cannot use the freedom to believe as a rationale to commit violence. Odd as it seems, abortionists talk religion all the time. While abortion was long spoken about as a decision "between a woman and her physician," we now hear it called a decision between "the woman, her physician, her family, her conscience, and her God." Which god is that exactly? One pro-choice bumper sticker declares, "Abortion—A Woman's Rite."

In her book *Why I Am an Abortion Doctor*, Suzanne T. Poppema wrote, "The reality is that our clinic is a relatively placid place. Some women add to this sense when they come in and stage what amounts to rituals around the procedures. A patient came in recently with her partner and brought candles, clearly making the experience a ritual way of saying, 'I am proud of myself for making this choice, but I'm also sad about the choice.'"[7]

Brenda Peterson wrote in the *New Age Journal* that abortion is a spiritual issue. She quoted Ginette Paris's book *Pagan Meditations*, in which Paris describes abortion as an essentially religious act, a sacred sacrifice to Artemis.[8] In her book *The Sacrament of Abortion*, Paris explains further that if we saw abortion as a sacred ritual, it would restore to the act "a sense of the sanctity of life."[9] The question remains: If we call abortion "a sacred ritual," can we trust that the Supreme Court decision against ritualistic human sacrifice would render abortion illegal?

Running out of rational arguments, abortion supporters take refuge in the court of final appeal: "This is between me and my God!"

The willingness to defend abortion on religious grounds despite evidence that the child is verifiably human reminds us of the Pharisees who steadfastly refused to believe in Jesus despite the evidence of the man born blind whose sight Jesus had miraculously restored.

Just as we cannot justify killing our neighbor with the excuse, "I did not believe he had a soul," so we cannot justify the killing of the child in the womb with the same rationale. The goal of the pro-life movement is not to impose our beliefs on anyone, but rather to protect the innocent from those who believe they can be killed. Abortion supporters are free to believe anything they want about the presence or the absence of a soul, but we do not want them to legislate their beliefs into a license to kill. Abortion is finally about bloodshed, not beliefs; about victims, not viewpoints.

PREACHING ABOUT POLITICS

On Sunday afternoon, March 21, 2010, a vote was scheduled in the United States Congress on the Patient Protection and Affordable Care Act, better known as Obamacare. Because it was a Sunday, and so many members of Congress are churchgoing Christians, they decided to hold a worship service that morning, right there in the U.S. Capitol, in Statuary Hall. I had received a call a few days earlier, asking if I could come and deliver a sermon, and I gladly did so.

In my remarks, I pointed out how Christ has transformed politics and centered it on the human person, whom He came to redeem. I reminded those members of Congress who had gathered that the most frequent admonition of Scripture is, "Be not afraid!" That doesn't just mean, "Don't worry; have courage." It means that we are called to welcome Jesus Christ and not worry whether He will deprive us of what we long for, not worry whether He will restrict our freedom or enslave our hopes. No, welcoming the Savior is precisely the fulfillment of our hopes and the foundation of our freedom!

I reminded them too that the message of the Savior served as the foundation of the representative form of government in which they played so crucial a role. In the pagan world before Christ, the ruler typically dictated government, and the people counted for little, if anything. But when Christ came, He taught that each individual had access to God and was called to share his or her very nature as a son or daughter of God the Father. That being true, no public official had the right to oppress other people. No legislator or governor, congress or court, could have a veto power over human rights. After Jesus, everyone counted, and therefore everyone had a voice. Power and authority become service. Legislators become ministers of God. And issues matter only because people matter more.

The theme I spoke of that day was explored beautifully by M. Stanton Evans in his book *The Theme Is Freedom*. He explained the pagan principle of government, as articulated by Greek and Roman philosophers and as codified in Emperor Justinian's sixth-century *Institutes*. "Whatever has pleased the prince," reads *Institutes*, "has the force of law, since the people . . . have yielded up to him all their power and authority." This philosophy later found voice in rulers like Richard II, king of England from 1377 to 1399, who said that the laws of England "were in his mouth." In the modern era, variations on the theme have emerged all over the world and share a common denominator: "That the law is the edict of the political sovereign of the moment. It is therefore limited by no exterior principle, but is exercised at the discretion of whoever happens to be in power, and thus can be changed at will when some new ruler gets on top."[10]

For all the wisdom of the ancient Greeks, Evans argued, they were not immune from the urge to absolutism. He quoted Aristotle to the effect that "when a whole family, or some individual happens to be so pre-eminent in virtues as to surpass all others, then it is just that they should be the royal family and supreme over all." Not one for halfway measures, Aristotle insisted that this king "should have the supreme power, and that mankind should obey him, not in turn, but always." According to Evans, this perspective was normative in pagan societies. Aristotle called these heroic figures "great-souled men." Plato called them "divine men" and "golden men," who had been ordained to rule above "the herd." "The monarch has an irrepressible authority (and is therefore not limited by consent)," said one Pythagorean writer quoted by Evans; "he is a living law; he is like a god among men."[11]

In a form of government like this, the people do not matter. The king says something, and it is law. The people have no input into the law's creation and no recourse against its execution. If the people are voiceless, if the individual is valueless, then an all-powerful state can dispose of these people as it pleases. This is how totalitarian regimes emerge and how holocausts happen. "When religious value is denied in the realm of spirit," Evans contends, "but reasserted in the secular order, dominion over every facet of life converges in a single center; the political regime becomes both church and state and claims authority over faith and conscience." He sees this "crushing, all-pervasive assertion of power" as the truly distinguishing feature of all totalitarian movements. It is, he says, "what makes totalitarianism 'total.'"[12]

Christ changes all this. He makes the human person count. He makes each human being a son or daughter of God and thereby breaks any claim of one human being to have absolute dominion over another. Christ revolutionizes politics. It is all centered now—or at least should be—on the divinely protected human person. So in speaking to Congress that day, I reminded those gathered that we don't just deal with the "issue" of health care. We deal with the people who need it. We don't just debate "immigration." We try to serve the needs of immigrants. We don't just argue about abortion. We serve the needs of the youngest children and their parents.

I reminded them that we always start with the dignity of the human person, realizing that human rights and dignity don't come from government and can't be taken away by government. If elected officials were the ones who decided whether people have their human rights, those wouldn't be *human* rights anymore. Human rights belong to humans because they are human, not because Congress decided to grant those rights. Therefore, we can rightly exclude no one from our service, our care, our protection.

"We come here today to worship God," I told the members of Congress, "because only through the worship of God can we understand fully our service to humanity. Only when we hear Christ say that He wants us to sit on His throne do we understand why we care about people." The destiny of these people, like ours, is the heights of heaven, sitting on God's throne. Given this shared destiny, I continued, we cannot turn the other way if our fellow humans are disposed of like garbage. We must understand that caring for the weak and the poor, including the unborn, cannot be the monopoly of one or another political party or held hostage to a partisan agenda. "In the voice of the helpless is the voice of God," I concluded, "and we are not free to exclude anyone."

This indeed is a message that needs to echo and reecho through the pulpits of America. The Church alone can best clarify the nature of politics. And the reason we are to preach about politics is not because the Church has become too political, but rather because our politics have become too pagan.

OUR GOD-GIVEN RIGHTS

In examining the Church's "no" to the state, we saw that part of what this means is that no state can demand our ultimate obedience. No human authority is ultimate over human beings.

Only God has total and ultimate authority over any human person. That is what we declare in the first line of the Nicene Creed: "We believe in one God." This is not just a statement that we believe in God. This is a statement that there is no other "god," and that we invest all authority in the one in whom we believe. That first line of the Creed is more powerful than a revolution. It is a statement to the world that anyone who claims any kind of authority, whether religious or secular, must submit to the one and only God. There is only one to whom we bend our knee. There is only one to whom we say, "Lord." There is only one whom we worship. There is only one for whom we would sacrifice our lives. It is one Lord, one God, one power, one authority, one dominion over all the earth.

As we have already seen, neither the Church nor we as individuals want to abolish the government. God gives us those who have legitimate authority over us. Yet, those who exercise that authority have to realize—and we have to realize too—that their authority is not ultimate. Only the authority of God is ultimate. Anybody who rules must also obey. Any law that is passed must also correspond to the law of God.

That is the beauty of our American system of government. We don't elect our leaders to do whatever they want to do, as if ours were a pagan form of government. Nor do we elect them to do whatever we want them to do, as if ours were a pure democracy, where majority rule trumped moral principles. Rather, we put our leaders in places of authority so they can carry out the moral law in regard to fundamental human rights and the protection of the common good as outlined in our founding documents.

That is why our Declaration of Independence says that we have our rights simply and precisely because we are human. This is why the Declaration so emphatically declares, "We hold these truths to be self-evident, that all men are created equal, that they are endowed by their Creator with certain unalienable Rights, that among these are Life, Liberty and the pursuit of Happiness." The Founding Fathers instituted government "to secure these rights." Our Creator did all the endowing.

We don't have the right to life because somebody else says that we have it. We don't have the right to life because some court, congress, governor, or king grants it to us. Rather, we have our rights from God. This is the fundamental understanding of our founding as a nation. And government exists to protect our God-given rights, not to parcel them out, and certainly not to take them away.

TWO

The World of *Roe*

IN MARCH 2005, I SAT BY THE BED OF A DYING WOMAN. THE night before she died, I was in her room for close to four hours, and then for another hour the next morning, her final hour. To describe the way she looked as "peaceful" is a total distortion of what I saw. For thirteen days, she had had no food or water. She was, as you would expect, terribly drawn in her appearance and declining visibly with every passing hour. Her eyes were open, but they moved restlessly from side to side, constantly darting back and forth. The best way I can describe the look on her face was *terrified sadness*.

The woman was Terri Schiavo. This unfortunate brain-injured woman died from court-enforced dehydration because her estranged husband decided her life was not worth saving.

One odd detail stands out in my memory of those days. There was a little night table in the room. I could put my hand on the table and on Terri's head all within arm's reach. And on that table was a vase of flowers filled with water. I looked at the flowers. They were fully nourished, living, beautiful. And I said to myself, "This is absurd, totally absurd. These flowers are being treated better than this woman. She has not had a drop of water for almost two weeks. Why are those flowers there? What type of hypocrisy is this?" The flowers were given water. Terri was not. Had I dipped my hand in that water and put it on her tongue, the officers standing around her bed would have led me out under arrest. Something was seriously wrong here.

In chapter 1, we looked at why Christians have a vital role to play in the public square. I described the intentions of our Founders and our responsibilities under the government they intended. But to move forward in the fight against abortion, we have to come to grips with a painful reality: we now have a different kind of government from what our Founders established, and that different kind of government has been established in no small part by the *Roe v. Wade* decision.

THE RADICAL BREAK

If we go back to *Roe v. Wade*, which legalized abortion in 1973, we do not see in that decision an assertion that the unborn are *not* human. The Supreme Court dodged that issue entirely. "We need not resolve the difficult question of when human life begins," said the decision. "When those trained in the respective disciplines of medicine, philosophy, and theology cannot arrive at any consensus, the judiciary, at this point in the development of man's knowledge, is not competent to speculate as to the answer."[1] But the decision continued, "The word 'person' as used in the Constitution does not include the unborn."[2] We need to understand what the justices were saying and what they were not saying. In essence, they were saying, "Yes, the child might be human—we can't say for certain—but we do have the authority to say you can kill it, regardless." Now, if the court had said, "We have concluded that the unborn are *not* human, and thus we acknowledge your right to abort them," this would have still been a wrong decision, but at least it would have preserved the principle that no government can authorize the killing of the innocent. But the justices did not preserve that principle. They subverted it. And when they subverted it, they established a different government than our Founding Fathers established.

We need to understand the seriousness of this reversal. What the Supreme Court said in *Roe* was, "We are now declaring that *we* the court, *we* the government of the United States, have the authority to remove some human beings from the protections of the Constitution. We have the authority to remove this protection not based on the humanity of the unborn, or lack thereof, but because *we* say so."

I don't think we as Americans have appreciated the absolutely radical break this decision represents. We tend to think that *Roe* was wrongly decided, that it introduced a bad and tragic policy, and that it has to be reversed. We also tend to think that because of *Roe* we will slide headlong down the slippery slope of evils that follow in its wake and end in a darker place than we can imagine. In fact, however, we are in that dark place. *Roe* put us there. It is hard to imagine much worse than the authorized killing of nearly 60 million innocents.

Where do we get totalitarian regimes? Where do we get holocausts? We get them from governments that somehow think *they* are the masters over life and death. When a government says that some people don't have to be protected, that is the stuff of which genocides are made. So when you hear a citizen or a candidate or a public servant or a congressman or a senator or a president or anybody say, "I think *Roe* was a good idea," he is not just telling you what he thinks about a medical procedure. He is telling you what he thinks about the authority of government: what kind of government he believes we have, and what kind of government he believes we ought to have.

It's time for us to change this. It's time for us to recall for ourselves, for our children, and for our grandchildren, what our history teaches—that we have a government based on certain principles that its leaders realize are beyond their authority and beyond their reach. Certainly, there are many other problems and concerns and issues. But we will never solve any of them if we allow this most fundamental injustice to continue.

THE VIOLATION OF PRINCIPLE

People can disagree about programs and policies while agreeing on basic principles. But to violate the principles themselves is a much more momentous problem.

For instance, we can agree on the principle that we have to help the poor. Solidarity with the poor is not only a matter of basic human rights; it is a repeated mandate in the Scriptures. We can disagree about the programs, the policies, the laws, the solutions to the problem; and the candidates do disagree with one another. Citizens disagree with one another. One says, "Here's the way we can solve it," and someone else comes along and says, "That program doesn't work. That actually is counterproductive. You should try my way." The disagreeing parties should argue it out. They should let trial and error have their say. As time goes by, we see what works best.

In the case of poverty, there is at least consensus on the principle. Christian values are aligned almost completely on this issue with progressive ones. We don't hear people saying, "The poor are less human than the rest of us and ought to be exterminated." No candidate would survive if he or she said that. No teacher would keep his classroom. No media person would keep her job. To recommend death for the poor, slow or quick, assaults an established principle: we have to help the poor. Of course we do. They are human beings. They deserve our help. We disagree on strategy but not on principle.

Abortion is different. When it comes to abortion, the policy *is* the principle. In other words, either these children have the right to live or they don't. Either we can round them up and kill them or we can't. The issue is open or shut, yes or no, black or white. It is not, "We agree on the principle. Now let's figure out different ways to get there." No, there is no way to say that abortion is acceptable without violating the principle. The very legality of abortion violates the principle.

It is as if one said, "Regarding the poor, not only do I not care about your program for helping them. I think that they should be killed." This is comparable to where we are when we speak about the "policy" on abortion. That policy attacks the entire moral order. It attacks the entire foundation of our government and strips every other human rights position of its very purpose.

RIGHT TO LIFE'S SINGULAR IMPORTANCE

Enabling the killing of innocents has altered the very foundation of our government. In *The Splendor of Truth* (1993), Pope John Paul II commented on the theme we are exploring here in these words:

> The root of modern totalitarianism is to be found in the denial of the transcendent dignity of the human person who, as the visible image of the invisible God, is therefore by his very nature the subject of rights which no one may violate—no individual, group, class, nation or State. Not even the majority of a social body may violate these rights, by going against the minority, by isolating, oppressing, or exploiting it, or by attempting to annihilate it.[3]

John Paul II elaborated on this thought in *The Gospel of Life* (1995). Governments, he said, have engaged in a comparable moral relativism. Rights are no longer based in the "inviolable dignity of the person," but rather are subject to the will of the stronger party. "The State is no longer the 'common home' where all can live together on the basis of principles of fundamental equality," he said, "but is transformed into a tyrant State, which arrogates to itself the right to dispose of the life of the weakest and most defenseless members." The state maintains the appearance of legality and the illusion of democracy, but this he saw as a "tragic caricature." The pope asked, "How is it still possible to speak of the dignity of every human person when the killing of the weakest and most innocent is permitted?"

When this is allowed to happen, the pope insisted, "the disintegration of the State itself has already begun." He concluded, "To claim the right to abortion, infanticide, and euthanasia, and to recognize that right in law, means to attribute to human freedom a perverse and evil significance: that of an absolute power over others and against others. This is the death of true freedom."[4]

These words from the pope place the abortion issue in a totally different category than just "one among many issues." They place it, rather, right at the very foundation of civilization and of the existence and purpose of government. A careful analysis shows the convergence of the pope's line of thought with that of our Founding Fathers, as expressed in the Declaration of Independence. The shared thought is that government exists for the people, and the rights of the people are based neither on the will of the people nor on the decision of those in power, but rather on their God-given human dignity. This is what the Declaration means by the word *unalienable*—the rights cannot be taken away ("alienated") either by the person him- or herself or by anyone else. Put another way, human rights are not granted by political systems. They are "pre-political." They exist before government and, in fact, must be honored, served, and secured by government, not because the leaders of government say so, but because to fail to do so undermines the very purpose of government.

This is the context in which we can also understand the assertion of Mother Teresa that the greatest destroyer of peace is abortion. In her Nobel Peace Prize acceptance speech of December 11, 1979, she said:

Many people are very, very concerned with the children in India, with the children in Africa where quite a number die, maybe of malnutrition, of hunger and so on, but millions are dying deliberately by the will of the mother. And this is what is the greatest destroyer of peace today. Because if a mother can kill her own child—what is left for me to kill you and you kill me—there is nothing between.[5]

Mother Teresa repeated these convictions in her speech to the National Prayer Breakfast in Washington, DC, on February 3, 1994, when she tied the practice of abortion to a negation of America's founding principles. After explaining how abortion subverts those principles, she exhorted those in attendance, including President and Mrs. Clinton, "If you become a burning light of justice and peace in the world, then really you will be true to what the founders of this country stood for."[6]

What those Founders stood for is the type of government that acknowledges that human rights belong to human beings *a priori*, precisely because God made them human. The legalization of abortion changes our government from one that protects unalienable rights to one that dispatches them as it sees fit.

The state must do more than tell us we have the right to life or assure us that its agents won't take our life. To honor our founding principles, the state must confer protection of that right. Martin Rhonheimer observes that the greatest threat for the unborn comes not from the state but from the mother. So if the state does not offer the unborn its active protection, the "right to life" would have no real meaning for the unborn or for defenseless infants. "The only means for the unborn to enjoy an effective right to life," argues Rhonheimer, "is through the state's guarantee to protect that life from private interference, from whomever may be interested in eliminating it." This right, says Rhonheimer, derives not from any particular quality or condition of the unborn, but rather from his or her simply "being a person."[7]

The right to life itself "occupies a singular place," Rhonheimer points out. Every other right depends on the right to life. Fighting poverty is important because the poor have a right to food, clothing, and shelter. They have a right to these material goods only because they have a right to life. Employment is an important issue because people have a right to make a living by their work, but they have a right to make a living only because they have a right to life. It's the foundation for everything else.

Because of its singular nature, George Weigel rejects the idea that the right to life is a uniquely Christian position being imposed on a pluralistic society. "[P]ublic officials who make that spurious claim," he insists in his book *Evangelical Catholicism*, "should be told politely, firmly, publicly, and relentlessly that they are wrong, and that their errors reflect ignorance, malice, or both." As the Church teaches, "the defense of the right to life is a matter of the first principles of justice that can be known by reason"; that is, it's universal.

Weigel says that those who talk about abortion as just another issue on par with the rest trivialize the debate. One's concerns about work, housing, education, health care, and the like can hardly make sense if life itself does not have to be protected. After all, if we don't have the right to live, we can hardly be said to have the right to enjoy the fruits of life. "The simple truth is," says Weigel, "if you are wrong on abortion, you can't be right on other issues."[8]

AN AMERICAN TAKEOVER OF AMERICA

In their 1998 national pastoral letter, *Living the Gospel of Life*, the United States Catholic bishops used some of the strongest and most startling language they have ever used. "When American political life becomes an experiment on people rather than for and by them, it will no longer be worth conducting," they said. "We are arguably moving closer to that day."[9]

With this language the bishops acknowledge that the disintegration of the state also means the disintegration of America, the failure of our great experiment in self-governance. The life debate is not just about "a bad policy." It is not even about a terrible policy. It is a debate about the very identity and survival of the nation.

Pro-abortion policies contradict not only the teachings of the Church but also the very idea of America itself. "In a striking way, we see today a heightening of the tension between our nation's founding principles and political reality," wrote the bishops. "We see this in diminishing respect for the inalienable right to life and in the elimination of legal protections for those who are most vulnerable. There can be no genuine justice in our society until the truths on which our nation was founded are more perfectly realized in our culture and law."

John Paul II spoke in strong but hopeful terms during his various visits to the United States. "This is the dignity of America, the reason she exists, the condition for her survival—yes, the ultimate test of her greatness," he told us in 1987, "to respect every human person, especially the weakest and most defenseless ones, those as yet unborn."[10]

In 1995, in an address given at Baltimore–Washington International Airport, he cited our founding documents and pleaded with us to recognize that at the heart of these documents "is the recognition of the rights of the human person, and especially respect for the dignity and sanctity of human life in all conditions and at all stages of development." He concluded, "I say to you again: America, in the light of your own tradition, love life, cherish life, defend life from conception to natural death."[11] To tolerate abortion not only flies in the face of Christian teaching. It is un-American.

This line of thinking reminds me of the press conference Priests for Life held at the National Press Club in Washington, DC, during the 2000 election. We were talking about the importance of electing pro-life candidates, and how the abortion issue surpasses all others because the fundamental purpose of government is to protect life.

During the question-and-answer session, a reporter said to me, "Father Frank, you are calling for a Vatican takeover of America."

A Vatican takeover of America?

"No," I said, "I'm calling for an American takeover of America!"

AN INTERNATIONAL RIGHT TO LIFE

Of course, because the principles we talk about here are based on natural law rather than any man-made law, they transcend America. The inherent right of human beings to the protection of their lives is acknowledged not only in the Declaration of Independence but in various international documents as well. After the horrors of World War II, people around the world realized that while individual nations have the duty to protect their citizens, such national protection does not always suffice. What happens if a nation's leaders turn against some of their own people? Who is responsible to intervene? To whom do those leaders and that nation answer?

The sense that there was a need for an international body to acknowledge and protect basic human rights, rights that individual nations can neither give nor take away, led to the development of the United Nations. The UN Charter, drafted in 1945, states that the purpose of the United Nations is "to reaffirm faith in fundamental human rights, in the dignity and worth of the human person."[12]

Within three years of its founding, the United Nations published the "Universal Declaration of Human Rights." According to this document, the "recognition of the inherent dignity and of the equal and inalienable rights of all members of the human family is the foundation of freedom, justice, and peace in the world."[13] Article 3 of the "Declaration" states, "Everyone has the right to life, liberty, and security of person." Article 6 elaborates, "Everyone has the right to recognition everywhere as a person before the law."

These words were certainly true in principle, but for them to have practical application, it was clear that more than a proclamation was needed. The substance of the "Universal Declaration" was therefore placed in hard legal form as an international treaty, the International Covenant on Civil and Political Rights, which the leaders of more than 160 nations have signed. This treaty states in Article 26, "All persons are equal before the law and are entitled without any discrimination to the equal protection of the law."[14]

In 1959, the United Nations further recognized basic human rights by issuing a "Declaration on the Rights of the Child." This declaration acknowledged that "the child, by reason of his physical and mental immaturity, needs special safeguards and care, including appropriate legal protection, before as well as after birth." This too was incorporated into a treaty, the Convention on the Rights of the Child (1989), which states in Article 6, "States Parties recognize that every child has the inherent right to life."[15]

To us in the pro-life movement, the next steps are obvious. As citizens of the world, we need to reconcile the language of these declarations and treaties and the needs they express with the reality of abortion, and the only way we can do that is by either scrapping the documents or abolishing abortion.

THREE

Time for Repentance

MANY FRIENDS ASK ME, "WHAT IS OUR FIRST SPIRITUAL DUTY regarding the abortion issue?" They think I'm going to answer, "Prayer." But actually, the answer is repentance. The first step in abolishing abortion is to examine our own hearts and to repent of the role we each have played in allowing this holocaust to happen. This is never easy, but with God's grace it can be done.

If anyone could speak to the depth of God's grace, it was Dr. Bernard Nathanson. A pioneer of the abortion industry and cofounder of the leading proabortion group NARAL, Nathanson oversaw the largest abortion clinic in the Western world and was responsible for some seventy-five thousand abortions. Nathanson eventually rejected the killing industry he helped to start, and at each stage of his turn to the light he was met with love and acceptance by the very pro-lifers he had once despised. In time, he became actively pro-life himself and converted to Christianity.

Dr. Nathanson was a strong supporter of Priests for Life. His reasoning was straightforward. He said that he and his colleagues would have never succeeded in starting the abortion industry if the clergy had been "united, purposeful, and strong." I visited Dr. Nathanson in his New York City apartment just days before he died. He was obviously weak. He could not lift his head from his pillow, nor could he raise his voice above a whisper. As I came into the room, the first thing he said to me, as I bent my ear close to his mouth, was, "Father Frank, how goes the crusade?"

This man, almost single-handedly responsible for launching the so-called abortion rights movement, was, to his last day, focused on undoing the damage he had done. His mind was not on his own illness and impending death, but on "the crusade," on the great cause of defending life, on the people who pledge their lives, fortunes, and sacred honor for their unborn brothers and sisters. When we engage, we convert. There is much more we can do to win the hearts and minds of those who advocate abortion.

RENOUNCING OUR COWARDICE

We begin our repentance by renouncing our cowardice, by regretting our silence, by rejecting our fear of risk and loss, our skewed priorities and attachments. Indeed, the fight against abortion does not start in the political arena or in the abortion clinics. The obstacles to a culture of life, and the enemies arrayed against it, are not primarily the massive funding of Planned Parenthood or the pervasive bias in the secular media. The biggest obstacles are inside of us. They are the lies we tell ourselves, the fears to which we willingly submit, and the pretense of ignorance about what we really have to do next.

Often, when people seek advice about pro-life activities, they ask me what they should do next. I start by telling them that they probably already know. Our sense of uncertainty rarely arises from not knowing what we should do. It arises from not having the courage to do it. We count the cost and don't want to pay the price. But it is time to risk, time to stand up and shout that the world is on fire— time to pull the fire alarm and join in the fight!

Martin Luther King Jr. raised this alarm, as he had already done so many times, on the night before he was assassinated. That evening he preached on the story of the good Samaritan (Luke 10:25–37). On the road from Jerusalem to Jericho, a man fell in with robbers. A priest and a Levite came by, but did not stop to help. Despite their knowledge of the Law and the Prophets, they walked right by. Why?

One of the reasons may be that they were afraid. The road from Jerusalem to Jericho is a steep and dangerous road that had come to be known as the "Bloody Pass." Because of its numerous curves, it lent itself to attacks by robbers, who could easily hide not too far from their victims. Perhaps the priest and Levite who passed by that man asked themselves, "If I stop to help this man, what will happen to me? Maybe the robbers who attacked him are still here. Maybe they're hiding just around the bend. This is a dangerous road. I better keep going."

Sometimes we ask a comparable question: "If I speak up too loudly about the victims of abortion, what will happen to me? Will I face persecution? Will I encounter opposition? Will I lose popularity if I get involved in a cause like this?" Pastors ask, "If I preach about abortion, what will happen to me? What will happen to my church, my effectiveness, my image? What legal troubles might I provoke?" Politicians ask, "If I say I am pro-life, what will happen to my votes, to my standing in the polls, to my chances in the election?" Business leaders ask, "If I take a stand against abortion, what will HR say? What will my customers say? How will it impact sales?" We all ask, in a million variations, "What will happen to me?"

And then the good Samaritan came along, and he reversed the question. He didn't ask, "If I help this man, what will happen to me?" He asked, "If I do not help this man, what will happen to him?" And that's the question for us. If I do not address this evil, what will happen to the unborn? If I do not get involved, what will happen to those who are vulnerable, to those who are marginalized, to those who are oppressed, to those who have no one to speak for them?

"I swore never to be silent whenever and wherever human beings endure suffering and humiliation," said Holocaust survivor Elie Weisel. "We must always take sides. Neutrality helps the oppressor, never the victim. Silence encourages the tormentor, never the tormented."[1]

ACCEPTING THE RESPONSIBILITY TO KNOW

In the 2008 presidential campaign, we were treated to the response of Barack Obama on the question of when a baby receives human rights. At the public forum at Saddleback Church in California, Obama said for the ages, "Whether you're looking at it from a theological perspective or a scientific perspective, answering that question with specificity is above my pay grade."[2] That, of course, is more or less what the Supreme Court said in *Roe v. Wade,* the decision that legalized abortion in America throughout all nine months of pregnancy.

This reminds us of what the Lord heard the first time a man killed another man, specifically, when Cain, son of Adam and Eve, killed his brother, Abel. As Genesis reports, the Lord confronted Cain and asked him, "Where is your brother?" Cain answered, "I do not know; am I my brother's keeper?" (Gen. 4:9). Cain dodged the question much as Obama and the court have. So what are we to think of those who speak this way? Is it vice or virtue? Do they display a careful effort not to play God, or a cowardly unwillingness to defend the rights of their fellow human beings?

Common sense tells us that if someone is hunting, and he doesn't know for sure whether what is moving behind the bush is a deer or a man, he should refrain from shooting until he does know. Doubt, in other words, leads to an abundance of caution, not to the abandonment of it.

Some say that the government should not be involved in the personal, private decision of abortion. They don't know how right they are. The government got too "involved" in the abortion decision when it legalized it. Despite its profession of ignorance about whether what is aborted is, in fact, a human life that has already begun, the court nevertheless declared, "The word 'person,' as used in the Fourteenth Amendment, does not include the unborn."[3] At which pay grade does a judge get the authority to define the boundaries of human rights or the limits of protection for the human family? Since when does the government get involved in deciding who qualifies for human rights?

Ignorance is not bliss. Claiming ignorance about who has human rights is a frightening abandonment of responsibility. Some may think it an exercise in humility not to "play God," but it is actually just the opposite. It is a claim *to be God*. We may claim not to decide, but in practice, we cannot escape deciding. Either we resolve to protect every human life, or we start deciding whom to exclude.

DISAGREEING TO AGREE

There are those who say we have the freedom to believe in the right to life but not the freedom to change public policy on this issue. They claim they are asking us to respect the freedom of others. But what they are really asking us to do is to be hypocrites. For example, if we clergy were to get up in the pulpit and say, "We have to be patient and kind with one another," and then rage at our fellow drivers on the way home, we would be accused of not practicing what we preach. Similarly, if we stood up in church and said, "We have an obligation to help the poor," and then cursed the homeless man begging outside the church door, we would be accused of hypocrisy and we *would* be hypocrites.

Some people—more than a few within the Church—ask us to be hypocrites on the subject of abortion. They tolerate us declaring from the pulpit, "We believe that God is the Giver of all life; the right to life comes from Him and cannot be infringed," and then they insist we stay mum on this issue once we leave church and enter the public square.

The solution that some propose to end the divisive controversy over abortion is simply for the opposing parties to "agree to disagree." This is presented as a reasonable option. It requires opponents not to change their views but rather to accept the views of others and, ultimately, the practices that flow from them. Sorry, but this is a proposal we in the pro-life movement can't accept.

First of all, to ask us to "agree to disagree" about abortion is to ask us to change our position on it. Why, after all, do we disagree in the first place? When we oppose abortion, we reject the notion that our position is negotiable. We do not only claim that *we* cannot practice it, but that *nobody* can practice it, precisely because it violates the most fundamental human right, the right to life. To "agree to disagree" means that we no longer see abortion for what it is—an act so violent and a human rights violation so fundamental that it defies compromise.

To "agree to disagree" is to foster the notion that the baby is a baby only if the mother thinks it is, that the child has value only if the mother says it does, and that we have responsibility only for those for whom we choose to have responsibility. Certainly, we can choose to "agree to disagree" about many issues. We can debate any number of proposals, programs, and strategies as we try to figure out how best to secure human rights and the general welfare. But these legitimate areas of disagreement relate to *how* to secure people's rights, whereas the abortion controversy is about *whether* to recognize those rights. "Agreeing to disagree" assumes neutrality about an issue, the right to life itself, in which neutrality is not an acceptable option.

Furthermore, the abortion dispute is not merely a policy disagreement. It is about justice. It is about violence, bloodshed, and the death of defenseless victims. In the face of a policy that permits thousands of babies to be killed every day, to "agree to disagree" eases the conscience of the killers and enables the sacrifice of the victims.

We don't fight oppression by "agreeing to disagree" with the oppressor. It is precisely when the oppressor disagrees that we have to intervene to stop the violence. The fact that the oppressor does not recognize the victim as a person does not remove our obligation to the victim. In the face of injustice, we are called not simply to disagree with it but to stop it. The proposal to "agree to disagree" presumes the issue is about people disagreeing over abortion, not about people being killed by abortion. The proposal shows how invisible the unborn victim remains. It is a false solution indeed.

THE ONE TO INTERVENE

Psychologists call the phenomenon the "bystander effect," and the case cited most often is that of Kitty Genovese. As the story goes, at 3:20 a.m. on a March morning in Queens, New York, Genovese, who managed a nearby bar, was attacked while walking toward her apartment building. She screamed that she had been stabbed. Lights of nearby apartments went on, windows opened, the attacker disappeared, but nobody came to help. Then the attacker returned, found his victim, and stabbed her again. She screamed, but nobody helped her or even called the police.

The attacker came back a third time. It was now a half hour later. He attacked and stabbed Kitty Genovese yet again, this time fatally. At that point the police received their first call and were there in two minutes, but they could not save Kitty's life.

In the days and weeks following this murder, detectives and reporters were distressed to learn that no fewer than thirty-eight people witnessed some part of this assault but did nothing. It was, they believed, an astonishing failure of human compassion and a stunning display of cowardice and apathy.

The witnesses were asked why they didn't help. Many did not want to talk. Some thought for sure that someone else was closer to the victim and would do something. The single individual who did call the police—a half hour after the attacks began—only did so after much deliberation and after having phoned a friend in Nassau County for advice, and then walked across the roof of the building to the apartment of an elderly woman in order to make the call. "I didn't want to get involved," this man told the police. Had the call come sooner, the police said, Kitty's life could have been saved.

The incident gave rise to debates among academics and research psychologists about what again came to be known as the "bystander effect." One of the psychological experiments conducted regarding the syndrome began with a man sitting in a room alone. Not knowing the experiment had already begun, he saw smoke pouring into the room from under the door of the next room. He immediately got up and alerted others that there was a problem. Later, three people were placed in that same room, and smoke began pouring in. They coughed and fanned the smoke away from their faces, but nobody got up or said anything.

The experiment showed that we don't just look at the evidence of an emergency. We look at the reactions of others. If they don't get excited, we reinterpret the data and conclude that things aren't as bad as they seem. The thirty-eight who witnessed Kitty's murder reinforced one another in their nonresponse. So it is with abortion. Individually, we see an emergency crying out for a massive response. Smoke pours in. Victims scream. Yet when we fail to see others respond, we doubt our own judgment and remain frozen in place. And like one of the Genovese witnesses, when asked why we did not get involved, so many of us simply say, "I don't know."

DEFENDING OUR SACRED HONOR

We have already seen how the tragedy of abortion strikes at the very foundation of our nation and of civilization. The right to life is pre-political. It belongs to us because we are human, period. It comes first. Government comes later. And that's one of the reasons why we can risk everything to defend it, because everything depends on it!

Our Founding Fathers understood this when they took their stand against King George and signed the Declaration of Independence. Signing this declaration was an act of high treason. The signers knew it was punishable by death. Short of that, they knew they could lose their property and their freedom. In fact, they did, some of them suffering imprisonment; physical harm; loss of homes, possessions, and family members; and even death. Yet not a one reneged on their pledge. As the signers showed, some causes are worth risking everything to defend. The right to life is one such cause.

The most daunting obstacle that stands between us and a culture of life is the fear in our own hearts. This fear leads us to doubt whether we really should risk everything and sacrifice all. And it is of this doubt and fear, this cowardice and hesitation, that we must repent today. In his book *Innocent Blood: Challenging the Powers of Death with the Gospel of Life,* John Ensor addresses the "self-preserving" instinct in human nature. Those who yield to it, like the priest and the Levite in the Samaritan parable, prefer the bliss of ignorance. "From within their fog," Ensor wrote, "both black and white can appear as any one of 1000 shades of gray." People of this mind-set, he argues, make a fetish out of the word *nuance.* They pride themselves on their sophistication, their ability to see distinctions that other people miss. Inevitably, nuance results in inaction and the preservation of the status quo.[4]

As the nation's founders made clear, not everyone yields to this prideful passivity. Ensor acknowledges an alternative set of people, those whose faith has given birth to courage and who recognize the imperative to mobilize, to act, to accept risk for the sake of the innocent. "God did not rescue us from sin and death to build a community of nervous chipmunks ever sniffing the air for potential danger," Ensor wrote. "He sealed our lives with his own death-defying Spirit so that we might act in kind."[5]

SHARING RESPONSIBILITY

The twenty-first chapter of Deuteronomy describes a ritual that God's people had to carry out when there was a slaying and the killer remained unknown. Scripture reads, "Your elders and your judges shall come forth, and they shall measure the distance to the cities which are around him that is slain." Those from the nearest city then needed to sacrifice a heifer, and their elders were to pray these words: "Our hands did not shed this blood, neither did our eyes see it shed. Forgive, O LORD, thy people Israel, whom thou hast redeemed, and set not the guilt of innocent blood in the midst of thy people Israel; but let the guilt of blood be forgiven them" (vv. 1–9).

What is going on here? Obviously, when innocent blood is shed, something happens in the land; something happens to the people in the land in their relationship to God, even if they are not the ones who shed the blood. As the account of the first murder makes clear, the innocent, though slain, still speak. "The voice of your brother's blood is crying to me from the ground," God told Cain (Gen. 4:10). God's people are bound up in an inescapable mutuality, a responsibility for one another that transcends their own choosing. We see again, in Isaiah 1, God telling His people, "Your hands are full of blood" (v. 15). These people had not done the killing, but because the killing occurred in their midst, they had a responsibility to intervene. Hence the passage continues with the instructions, "Seek justice, correct oppression" (v. 17).

What of us? Our land is polluted with the innocent blood of tens of millions of aborted children. The fact that we ourselves have not done the killing does not absolve us of responsibility. We know where the killing occurs. We know how it is done, and we know who is doing it. Abortion is publicly advertised and advocated. Because it occurs in our midst, we are inescapably involved and inevitably more responsible than those people of the Book who simply had a murder committed in their midst.

What, then, are we to do? We need to repent. We need to see abortion not just as somebody else's sin but as our sin. Even if we have never participated in an abortion, we must ask forgiveness for it. It is easy to blame abortion on those who do it and support it. But we must blame ourselves as well. This is a spiritual dynamic that has to undergird all of our other activities to abolish abortion. First and foremost we are called to repent, to take responsibility for the innocent blood that has been shed, and then to intervene to save the helpless.

Fortunately, the blood of another innocent victim shows us the way. Jesus' blood "speaks more graciously than the blood of Abel," we learn in Hebrews 2:24. Let us repent of abortion, wash ourselves in Jesus' blood, and get to work defending the innocent.

KNOWING THE SOURCE OF LOVE

Ultimately, what defines this work, as well as the goal of the repentance to which we are called, and the sacrifices we make, is love—love in the very specific, historical context of the sacrifice of Jesus Christ. What He did foreshadows what we are to do. Saint John spelled this out clearly, and it has direct application to our fight for our unborn brothers and sisters.

"We know that we have passed from death to life, because we love our brothers," wrote John. "Anyone who does not love remains in death. Anyone who hates his brother is a murderer, and you know that no murderer has eternal life in him." John also told us how we have come to understand the potential of love. Said he, "This is how we know what love is: Jesus Christ laid down his life for us. And we ought to lay down our lives for our brothers. If anyone has material possessions and sees his brother in need but has no pity on him, how can the love of God be in him?" (1 John 3:14–17 NIV).

Note here that our responsibility to our brothers and sisters, including the youngest among them, is spelled out simply and clearly:

we are to lay down our lives for them. This is love, and it is not simply a commandment, but a way of life given to a community by the One who exemplifies it. He gave His life, and we have life as a result, and that life binds us together in a community marked by our willingness to lay down our lives. The ancient saying of Tertullian about the early Christians comes to mind: "See how they love one another, and how they are ready to die for each other."[6] The second part of the statement, which clarifies what the first part means, is often left out.

The pro-life commitment is simply the living out of this commandment, of this love, as applied to the children in the womb. Our resistance to unjust laws in this regard is not simply to disobey a command to participate in the killing of those children. It is rather to refuse to let the state or anyone else put a cap on our love. We cannot be commanded to love the unborn "only a little bit" or "up to this point and no further." When we love them, we will serve them and save them, despite the law that tells somebody else that they may kill them.

The first Christians were able to live this command of love, as Saint John went on to explain, because the source of that love, the Christ who sacrificed Himself, was personally known to them. They saw and touched the evidence that we pass from death to life when we love and sacrifice out of that love. They saw the risen Lord, touched Him, heard Him, and therefore proclaimed Him out of love, even when commanded not to, and even when it would cost them their lives. Wrote John, "That which was from the beginning, which we have heard, which we have seen with our eyes, which we have looked at and our hands have touched—this we proclaim concerning the Word of life. The life appeared; we have seen it and testify to it" (1 John 1:1–2 NIV).

This truth was repeated in Acts when Peter and John insisted, "We cannot help speaking about what we have seen and heard" (4:20 NIV).

This contact with the humanity of the Christ who loved them and gave Himself for them speaks to us of what we are to do now for the unborn. It is the contact with the human reality of their lives, and the human tragedy of their deaths, that is to impel us in our self-sacrificing love for them. It is not the "nuance" of the super-sophisticated that inspires self-sacrificing, life-giving action. It is contact with the humanity we serve. It is facing the injustice that casually takes human life and making a human response to it, a response that springs from the depths of our own humanity, a response inspired by the love of the God who gave that humanity to us. It is repenting for our past failures to act. And it is understanding that God will both forgive our failures and enable our victories.

FOUR

The Irrepressible Spiritual Imperative

DESPITE BEING BORN INTO A WEALTHY AND ACCOMPLISHED family, Basil of Caesarea put his worldly reputation on the line and worked against abortion and infanticide in the fourth-century Roman Empire. In his history of the pro-life movement, *Third Time Around,* George Grant tells how Basil's passion for life drove him and his colleagues to dismantle a Caesarean shrine to infanticide despite potential retaliation by the authorities. Fortunately, Basil's valor sufficiently impressed Emperor Valentinian that he would soon criminalize child-killing. "All parents," the emperor decreed, "must support their children conceived; those who brutalize or abandon them should be subject to the full penalty prescribed by law."

Basil felt compelled by, as Grant calls it, "an irrepressible spiritual imperative."[1] It's the same imperative Peter showed in Acts: "We cannot help speaking about what we have seen and heard" (see Acts 4:18–20 NIV).

That spirit has not died. Former Kansas attorney general Phill Kline was among those contemporary political figures who understood the imperative. In a hostile environment, he filed thirty fully warranted criminal charges against late-term abortionist George Tiller and 107 criminal charges against Planned Parenthood. For his efforts, the media savaged Kline. His weak-kneed friends abandoned him. With the ground softened, his political enemies drove him out of office, dropped both sets of charges, and started harassing him through the courts. Kline has had to surrender his law license in the interim, but like Basil, like the Founding Fathers, he never surrendered his sacred honor.

HOLY IMPATIENCE

One of the most helpful words in the English language is *empathy*, the feeling that we understand and share another person's experiences and emotions. Empathy is part of what drives the imperative. Consider too the case of William Wilberforce, the catalyst in Britain's abolition of the slave trade. Wilberforce gave the "Abolition Speech" to Parliament in 1789, and in that speech revealed this human, spiritual imperative that took hold of him and made his commitment to abolition absolute:

> As soon as ever I had arrived thus far in my investigation of the slave trade, I confess to you sir, so enormous, so dreadful, so irremediable did its wickedness appear that my own mind was completely made up for the abolition. A trade founded in iniquity, and carried on as this was, must be abolished, let the policy be what it might, let the consequences be what they would, I from this time determined that I would never rest till I had effected its abolition.[2]

Observe how Wilberforce's commitment is rooted not in some abstract "nuance" but in a concrete, human connection with the victims. This connection did not lead Wilberforce to despair but rather to a determination that he "would never rest." In 1793, at a low point in the abolition efforts, Wilberforce again asserted in a letter that irrepressible spiritual imperative. "[I]n the present instance where the actual commission of guilt is in question, a man who fears God is not at liberty," wrote Wilberforce. "If I thought that the immediate Abolition of the Slave Trade would cause an insurrection in our islands, I should not for an instant remit my most serious endeavors."[3]

Three years later, Wilberforce made another motion for abolition in Parliament. Weary colleagues called for "suspending the question" until the end of the year. Wilberforce responded, "The question suspended! Is the desolation of wretched Africa suspended? Are all the complicated miseries of this atrocious trade—is the work of death suspended?" No, Wilberforce would not delay the motion, and he called upon the House "not to insult the forbearance of Heaven" by dragging its feet.[4]

We see too the expression of the irrepressible spiritual imperative in Martin Luther King Jr.'s "Letter from a Birmingham Jail." King wrote this treatise in response to some concerned clergymen who questioned his timing, particularly in terms of direct action. "Frankly, I have yet to engage in a direct-action campaign that was 'well-timed' in the view of those who have not suffered unduly from the disease of segregation," wrote King. "For years now I have heard the word 'Wait!' It rings in the ear of every Negro with a piercing familiarity. This 'Wait' has almost always meant 'Never.'"

One can almost see the imperative flowing from the ink in King's letter. "There comes a time," he concluded, "when the cup of endurance runs over, and men are no longer willing to be plunged into the abyss of despair. I hope, sirs, you can understand our legitimate and unavoidable impatience."[5]

The champions of nuance are content with the status quo. Great moral leaders are not. We see this streak of impatience in all of them. We will end abortion when enough of us grow restless, when we connect, both mentally and emotionally, with the human tragedy abortion represents, when we drink deeply of that spiritual imperative and become inebriated with holy impatience.

NO MORE RATIONALIZATION

Unfortunately, not enough of our pro-life colleagues share the restless commitment to action displayed by Basil, Wilberforce, and King. Too many of us conduct the abortion fight on a level too abstract to overcome the instinct of self-preservation that kicks in when action involves risk. Once we are forced to choose between protecting the unborn and protecting our power and prestige, we start plotting an exit strategy.

We don't change our position on abortion. It is not that kind of compromise. We rationalize that by protecting our reputation we will be better able to fight the evil of abortion down some imaginary road. However sincere, this is pure rationalization. When the rationalizers prevail, what really needs to get done never gets done. We find ourselves in the realm of "nuance." Suddenly, we are too like the apostle Peter when he told Jesus, "God forbid that this should happen to you!" (Matt. 16:22, paraphrased).

The battlefield is no place for the overly cautious. Everywhere we turn in this battle, we see the inevitability of sacrifice. To make the smallest steps forward for the unborn, we have to give up something. I recall a conversation with a well-known Catholic vocalist who told me that the mention of the unborn in a modern Catholic song, which you would recognize, was kept there only after great struggle. Too often, pro-life groups who wish to bring a speaker to Christian schools and churches face pushback from authorities who insist the speaker "talk about all the issues" (not just abortion). On what other topic do organizers face this kind of resistance? I know this from my own experience. On more than one occasion, a diocese has shut me out because a few people objected that I have been "too aggressive on abortion."

I am proud to have provoked that objection. History will show how completely appropriate such "aggression" is. If I have a concern, it is that I have not been forward enough. The time is now for all of us to be so, to take the stands that need to be taken, to say the things that need to be said, and to sacrifice the things that need to be sacrificed to bring this abortion holocaust to an end.

DOUBLETHINK AND BLIND SPOTS

There is a tremendous disconnect at every level of our society regarding abortion, and as a result, the child in the womb has become the great blind spot of our culture. This disconnect is fueled by denial and fraught with the most blatantly absurd contradictions that the human mind can conjure. To advance justice for the unborn, we have to challenge these contradictions and expose them. We begin by examining some widely held principles that would seem to protect the unborn but that are not applied to them.

On February 28, 2006, the office of U.S. Congresswoman Rosa L. DeLauro sent out a press release saying, "House Democrats Release Historic Catholic Statement of Principles: Expresses Commitment to Dignity of Life and Belief That Government Has 'Moral Purpose.'" Whatever else was "historic" about it, it was one of the most profound examples of disjointed thinking on the abortion issue ever published. The fact is that the fifty-five Democrats who signed the document have for the most part voted consistently to deprive children in the womb of their most fundamental right, life itself.

Yet while voting for policies that permit, expand, and even fund the dismemberment of living children, these Catholic Democrats had the nerve to declare, "We are proud to be part of the living Catholic tradition—a tradition that promotes the common good, expresses a consistent moral framework for life, and highlights the need to provide a collective safety net to those individuals in society who are most in need. As legislators, in the U.S. House of Representatives, we work every day to advance respect for life and the dignity of *every* human being." And then, most unbelievably, they say, "We are committed to making real the basic principles that are at the heart of Catholic social teaching: helping the poor and disadvantaged, protecting the most vulnerable among us."[6]

The most vulnerable among us? The only human beings in our

nation today to be considered "nonpersons" also happen to be the youngest, the smallest, and the most dependent. If they are not "the most vulnerable among us," then who is? And by what twisted logic is voting to keep legal those procedures that tear these children apart consistent with "protecting" them? Something is radically wrong here. To talk about the dignity of life and the protection of the vulnerable while advancing the abortion industry agenda is a textbook example of what George Orwell called "doublethink,"[7] the embrace of two contradictory ideas at the same time. Yet a significant number of the members of the highest lawmaking body in the United States have been doublethinking their way through life and getting away with it for years. It is time to call them out.

There is indeed a distinction between two different groups of abortion advocates, the propagandists on the one hand and the practitioners on the other. The practitioners see the women crying and screaming. They deal with the bloody parts of little babies. They cope with the literal stench of death. Of the two groups, the propagandists succeed more readily in the rationalizing necessary to support legal abortion. The reason is simple: they don't see abortions. Nor do they deal with the devastating results for child and parents. The practitioners, on the other hand, see the concrete evidence every day, and it is harder for them to deny. That is why they are more willing to talk with us on the pro-life side. They know we see what they see.

But for the propagandists things are a lot cleaner and simpler: they send out press releases; hold press conferences; prepare reports in cushy offices; and talk about freedom, rights, and choices. One thing the propagandists rarely discuss, however, is what an abortion actually is. For them it's a concept, not a killing. As I have often said, the last thing supporters of abortion want to discuss is *abortion*. You will not hear them describe the procedure or any of its gory details. Often they avoid the very word, instead couching it in softer, more acceptable terms like "a woman's right to choose" or "reproductive rights."

We are living in a world proud to turn a blind eye to the obvious. That great blind spot in our culture covers the children in the womb. Our mission is to shine light on that darkness.

ENDING THE DISCONNECT

Soon after the December 2012 shooting in Sandy Hook Elementary School in Newtown, Connecticut, Dr. Keith Ablow of Fox News published an opinion piece titled "Who Would Kill Children?" He expressed, of course, the outrage of all but the most callous of our citizens that a shooting like this could occur.[8] Even the abortion-supporting President Obama expressed his anger, lamenting the lost futures of these children. As to the question, though, of who would kill children, the answer is simple. We would. Twenty children were killed in Sandy Hook. On average, twenty unborn children are killed every day in the ten minutes it took Adam Lanza to kill those innocent kids in Connecticut. And we permit it.

Television commentator Melissa Harris-Perry, remarking on the controversial case of the slain teenager Trayvon Martin, observed that the verdict left the impression that it was "okay to kill an unarmed African American child who has committed no crime."[9] Yet every day more than a thousand African American children are killed in the womb. Apparently it's more than an impression that this is "okay."

There exists a serious disconnect in the way people perceive social issues. I got a sense of this on the beautiful, sunny morning of May 17, 2009, when I spoke on the campus of the University of Notre Dame. President Obama spoke there that day too. It was Commencement Day, but that year there were two simultaneous ceremonies. At the larger one, the president received an honorary law degree. At the smaller one, I spoke to the students who refused to honor a president who is firmly committed to legal abortion. These students, with the "precious feet" of the unborn child image on their caps, embodied the irrepressible spiritual imperative and that readiness to sacrifice of which we have been speaking.

The president, for his part, unwittingly embodied the great disconnect. "If there is one law that we can be most certain of," he said, "it is . . . the Golden Rule—the call to treat one another as we wish to be treated."[10] For the president, however, that "one law we can be most certain of" remains uncertain in its application to the unborn. Somehow he, like all supporters of abortion, does not feel bound to treat those children the way he would want to be treated. Who, after all, would volunteer to be "treated" to being dismembered by abortion?

In an attempt to undercut Christian teaching, Obama called on the students to keep an open mind about what their faith tells them regarding abortion. "Faith," he said, "necessarily admits doubt." That, presumably, in the mind of the president, is the open door to the "nuance" that allows sophisticated leaders like him to favor legal abortion. Some doubt about the "definitive knowledge" of the rights of the unborn must be allowed, he claimed. But then Obama referred to the anniversary of *Brown v. Board of Education*, which rightly has personal significance for him, and all nuance disappeared. What would be the margin of "doubt" that the president would advocate regarding that decision to end school segregation? Understandably, there should be no doubt about civil rights for people of color. Yet for children in the womb, the doubt persists, and the disconnect continues.

Priests for Life has been strengthening its natural connection to the civil rights movement through the work of Dr. Alveda King, the niece of Martin Luther King Jr. Her father, Rev. A. D. Williams King, was Martin's brother. She began working with me full-time as our director of African American outreach in 2004. She and I have been together with her family at many events both happy and sad, including the annual observances of the national Martin Luther King Jr. holiday at Ebenezer Baptist Church in Atlanta, and the fiftieth anniversary celebration of the "I Have a Dream" speech at the Lincoln Memorial in Washington, DC.

On these occasions, we have been privileged to hear some of the most soaring oratory about justice, equality, and freedom ever voiced. Time and time again, I have been energized by these speeches and moved to recommit myself to the pursuit of justice and equality for every human being. But it is precisely in these settings that the disconnect is most pronounced. Speaker after speaker evokes the deepest human emotion about violence in the streets, social inequities, economic injustice, and the horrors of war—to mention a few—but these leaders fail conspicuously to speak of the need to secure justice and equality for the unborn child.

Alveda and I have both felt the disconnect so intensely at these gatherings that, amid the loud applause, we sometimes say out loud, "And the children too! Don't forget the children in the womb!" We were indeed gratified when, on a single occasion, the MLK Holiday observance at Ebenezer in January 2013, the Reverend Samuel Rodriguez, in his keynote address, mentioned the need to protect all life, including life in the womb. That is the kind of consistency that gives credibility to the cry for justice and equality in all the other contexts that are mentioned.

In an effort to overcome this disconnect, Alveda and some other members of her family have signed onto a declaration that her mother read publicly in Washington, DC, and placed in a time capsule under the new monument of Dr. King. It is a declaration saying that the "Beloved Community" of which Dr. King preached and for which he labored and died must include the children in the womb. Justice is not justice if some injustice is still permitted; equality is not equality if some are still not equal; and nonviolence is not non-violence if some violence is still allowed. We all know this; let the disconnect come to an end.

EXCLUDE NO ONE

"The innocents whom God has commanded us to care about are precisely the kind of people we are apt to overlook—and would prefer to overlook."[11] Those are the words of my friend John Ensor, in his compelling book *Innocent Blood.* As I have learned the hard way, that mind-set threatens us all.

Those of us who defend life are sometimes treated with the same disrespect for life as the unborn and the disabled are. In my own case, I have had to have special federal protection, even bodyguards, at some of the events at which I have spoken because of threats to my life. That's what happens when you identify with victims whom the world considers disposable. You become disposable in their eyes too.

We strike against this mind-set by showing a love for human life that is indivisible and that excludes nobody, not those who oppose us, not even those who take life as casually as we might take a walk. As John Paul II wrote, "Not even the murderer loses his personal dignity."[12] In that spirit, I recommend that we all engage those on the other side of the abortion issue, even to the point of initiating dialogue with practicing abortionists and ardent abortion advocates. Every abortionist is a human being whose life is worth protecting and whose soul is worth saving.

Among my friends is Mr. Bill Baird, known by the dubious title the "Father of the Pro-Choice Movement." Baird has three Supreme Court case victories to his credit, including the case that legalized contraception for single people. He was a pioneer of "reproductive rights." He would come year after year to the National Right to Life Convention to do opposition research and picket the convention hotel. Despite our obvious differences, he and I began to talk, and over the years established a relationship of authentic dialogue and mutual concern.

I remember him attending the Masses I celebrated for those National Right to Life Conventions, and at the conclusion of one such Mass, I said to him publicly, "Bill, we respect your life as much as we respect the life of the unborn child." Everyone applauded. He told me he had never been respected like that before. This is the only way we break through to some of these people. They will learn our message of "respect for *every* human life" when they see that we respect their lives too.

FIVE

Freedom of Speech

NOW THAT WE HAVE ESTABLISHED OUR RIGHT TO ENTER THE public square and the imperative to engage the opposition once there, we need to know what our rights are therein. This exercise is not as obvious as it seems. There are forces afoot in the land that will try to limit what we can say and do, and many of these forces are within our own churches.

To no earthly subject, however, do we give more importance than life itself, and thus our freedom to defend this subject is fundamental and inarguable. When, in fact, we speak in defense of life, we move beyond speech to action. Our very speech becomes an act of justice, an intervention to save the helpless. Speech in defense of life shares in a particular way that characteristic of God's Word whereby it accomplishes what it signifies: speaking of life can actually save lives! We can conclude from all this that both the Church and the state have the obligation to protect the freedom to speak in defense of life either from a civic or religious perspective.

Our fight for our unborn brothers and sisters is a fight for freedom and against tyranny. Our Founding Fathers fought this fight, and so must we, with the same readiness for self-sacrifice. This is true for every American and all the more true for us as disciples of the Lord Jesus Christ. The Gospel is a Gospel of freedom. "It is for freedom that Christ has set us free" (Gal. 5:1 NIV). The Christian is at the service of a heavenly kingdom that embodies the essence of freedom. The Church, carrying out the mission of Christ Himself, is dedicated to promoting freedom. "I have come to proclaim liberty to the captives . . . to let the oppressed go free," Jesus said in defining His mission. (See Luke 4:17–19.)

Carrying out this mission requires the freedom to speak the truth as we understand it. Not only was this fundamental right explicitly acknowledged by our Founding Fathers in the very first amendment to the Constitution, but it has also been affirmed time and time again by the Supreme Court. In the 1964 case *New York Times Co. v. Sullivan*, the court asserted that the right of citizens to advocate for particular issues reflects our "profound national commitment to the principle that debate on public issues should be uninhibited, robust, and wide-open."[1]

In the landmark *Citizens United v. Federal Election Commission* case in 2010, the Supreme Court affirmed in regards to speech affecting elections, "Speech is an essential mechanism of democracy, for it is the means to hold officials accountable to the people. The right of citizens to inquire, to hear, to speak, and to use information to reach consensus is a precondition to enlightened self-government and a necessary means to protect it."[2]

The corresponding freedom of the Church to speak and teach the truth, confirmed in the Bill of Rights' freedom of religion clause, is mandated by the Church as well. This freedom is, in fact, implicit in the Great Commission left by Jesus Christ: "Preach the gospel to every creature" (Mark 16:15 KJV). And: "Teach them to carry out everything I have commanded you" (Matt. 28:20, paraphrased). Because the Gospel covers every aspect of human activity, the Church must be free to comment on political matters—particularly when human rights are on the line. It would be the gravest irresponsibility not to.

UNDERSTANDING THE TAX CODE

If the devil is really in the details, in no set of details is he more active than those that make up our tax code, especially in the context of elections.

The federal laws of the United States take their origin, as I have noted, from two founding documents, the Declaration of Independence and the Constitution. The Declaration expresses the principles at the heart and soul of our system of government. This is the document that identifies the right to life as primary and unalienable, given by God, and secured by government. The Constitution is the "how to" document, the practical mechanism by which a system based on these principles can work. This document tells us how laws are to be made and what the respective roles of Congress, the president, and the courts are. All of these branches of government, and all the laws that flow from them, are to correspond with their foundation expressed in the Declaration and the Constitution.

The federal laws of the United States are organized in the Code of Laws of the United States of America (the "U.S. Code"). The Code has some fifty-one sections, called "titles," which deal with subjects such as the president, Congress, commerce, trade, and so forth. One of those sections, Title 26, the Internal Revenue Code (IRC), deals with tax issues. Note that the IRC is distinct from the IRS (Internal Revenue Service). The IRC refers to a set of federal laws. The IRS refers to a government agency, a bureau of the Department of the Treasury, responsible for collecting taxes and for interpreting and enforcing the IRC. As we will see in more detail later, the interpretations put forth by this agency are not law.

This is the uncertain legal terrain on which the battle to speak freely is being fought. The battle has focused here precisely because of limitations placed on what churches, organizations, and individuals can say and do regarding elections. For us, one goal is to cut through the fog of legal warfare and eliminate the confusion regarding what those limitations are, how much weight they really carry, and whether they align with the documents that are at the foundation of all American law. Moreover, as far as the Church is concerned, it is crucial to clarify how these limitations correspond, if at all, with the Church's understanding of her own nature, mission, and ultimate loyalties.

Let's begin by looking at what limitations we are talking about and how they came into being. Then we will look at how they are interpreted and misinterpreted by bureaucratic agencies of both the government and the Church. First, we have to understand that the limitations we discuss here are ones that the law requires for organizations if they are to be considered exempt from paying federal income tax. For many organizations this is not an issue, as they choose not to be exempt.

Other organizations, including most churches, apply for tax-exempt status from the government. They define their mission and activities in such a way that they can assert, through the appropriate government forms, that they qualify for tax-exempt status. The government then issues a ruling or determination letter indicating that the organization is tax-exempt.

In the tax-exempt category, there are two basic classifications. Organizations created according to the criteria in section 501(c)(3) of the Internal Revenue Code tend to focus their activity on *education*. They are allowed to do some lobbying—meaning advocacy for a particular piece of legislation—but are not allowed to do any "political intervention." By contrast, organizations created according to the criteria in section 501(c)(4) tend to focus their activity on lobbying and are allowed to do *some* political intervention.

Then we come to churches. What may come as a surprise for many is that churches are *not* tax-exempt because of a form they fill out and a letter of determination that they receive from the government. Rather, churches are automatically tax-exempt by law. Whether they seek a determination of that status from the government by filling out a form and receiving a letter is entirely up to their leadership. But even without the documentation, churches remain exempt as long as their mission corresponds to the criteria of tax-exempt entities. As the federal courts confirmed in *Branch Ministries v. Rossotti*, "Although most organizations seeking tax-exempt status are required to apply to the Internal Revenue Service for an advance determination that they meet the requirements of section 501(c)(3), id. § 508(a), a church may simply hold itself out as tax exempt and receive the benefits of that status without applying for advance recognition from the IRS."[3]

The tax exemption of churches actually dates back to ancient times. As the Supreme Court itself has noted, there is an "unbroken" history of such exemption in our country, and it "covers our entire national existence and indeed predates it." As Erik W. Stanley pointed out in an article on which I will rely heavily in this chapter, "[T]he unassailable fact remains that, for as long as anyone can remember, churches have always been tax-exempt or enjoyed favorable tax treatment." The article refers to examples of the tax exemption of religious institutions from ancient Sumeria in 2800 BC on forward.[4]

This exemption is understandable from the perspective of our own Constitution and from a consideration of the nature of the Church. "My kingdom is not of this world," the Lord said (John 18:36 ESV). The Church represents the intrusion into history of the Kingdom of God. Good Christians are called to be good citizens. These roles are not necessarily incompatible, but neither are they identical. That is why the Church does not seek permission for its mission from civil government. Nor does our Constitution presume the authority to give such permission. Hence the First Amendment declared, "Congress shall make no law respecting an establishment of religion, or prohibiting the free exercise thereof."

So churches are tax-exempt by law. Most of them take the additional step of seeking a letter of determination from the government, and most will organize their activities under the umbrella of 501(c)(3). But they do not have to do that. A church could choose to organize some of its activities under the (c)(3) umbrella and others under the (c)(4) model, or even organize an LLC, a *limited liability corporation*, or an LLP, a *limited liability partnership*, thus allowing additional freedom.

CUTTING THROUGH THE CONFUSION

It would be useful to look at some of the requirements in the law for maintaining tax-exempt status under section 501(c)(3). This is where confusion reigns supreme. Unfortunately, as we shall soon see, there is little clarification to be had.

By way of background, two limitations were added to the Internal Revenue Code (IRC), one in 1934 and one in 1954, restricting certain activities of nonprofit organizations and churches. The history of both of these limitations shows that they were shaped by no loftier motive than the self-interest of individual politicians.

In 1934, a provision was added to the code saying that an entity would not be recognized as tax-exempt if a "substantial part of . . . [its] activities . . . is carrying on propaganda, or otherwise attempting, to influence legislation." This is not an absolute prohibition on lobbying, but an indication that a 501(c)(3) must keep the bulk of its activities focused on education, religion, and the related actions that define a charitable purpose. "Interestingly," wrote Stanley, "the original version of the proposed 1934 bill included a ban on tax-exempt organizations' 'participation in partisan politics,' but that provision was removed in conference out of fears that it was too broad."[5] As Stanley points out, Senator David Reed, a Republican senator from Pennsylvania, sponsored the 1934 lobbying restriction to silence the nonprofit National Economy League with which he was sparring over the issue of veteran benefits. This kind of petty conflict did an injustice to the Declaration, the carefully hammered-out practical wisdom of the Constitution, and the relevant statutes of the United States Code.

In 1954, political self-interest again inspired a new legal restriction. At the time, Senate majority leader Lyndon B. Johnson of Texas added an amendment to Section 501(c)(3) that would limit tax-exempt status under this section to an organization "which does not participate in, or intervene in (including the publishing or distributing of statements), any political campaign on behalf of any candidate for public office."[6]

Having won his Senate seat by a margin of only eighty-seven highly disputed votes and now up for reelection, Johnson wanted to silence two secular, nonprofit organizations that were supporting his opponent. Johnson had made inquiries with the IRS commissioner to determine whether these organizations were breaking any law by their political involvement. When told they were not, he introduced the amendment to punish them for what had been legal up until then. At the time, there were no discussions, debates, or any considerations of a constitutional foundation for the amendment. Nor was there any discussion as to whether this restriction applied to churches. In fact, as Stanley points out, Johnson aide George Reedy maintained that "Johnson would never have sought restrictions on religious organizations."[7] The amendment was taken into committee and was adopted as the House and Senate versions of the tax reform were being reconciled.

And that seems to be the long and short of it—an amendment, as Stanley says, that "appears to be nothing more than an attempt by a powerful senator to silence political opponents that he feared were hurting his chances for reelection."[8] It should be noted that in 1987 the words "in opposition to" were added to this amendment, so that it now reads "any political campaign on behalf of or in opposition to any candidate for public office." Believe it or not, that addition also was motivated by the self-interest of other politicians seeking to silence nonprofit organizations. Such is the history of the Johnson Amendment, which is still law to this day.

When we turn to the actual content and substance of the tax law, we begin to see additional reason for concern. What exactly does the law mean? How does one know how to apply it and where to draw the lines or define the terms? For instance, how is one to define who is a "candidate" and which positions are meant by "public office"? Furthermore, what exactly is meant by "participate in" and "intervene in"? In order to observe a law, one has to know what behavior it does or does not prohibit. If a law is too vague, or extends to behavior beyond what it is specifically trying to target, it becomes unconstitutional.

As noted earlier, it is the IRS that is tasked with interpreting the Internal Revenue Code (IRC), which includes the Johnson Amendment. The IRC is law; the IRS interpretation is not. But the IRS interpretation of this political activity prohibition has been less than helpful. In fact, it has been a maze of confusion and inconsistency that, in practice, has made this provision unintelligible and therefore next to impossible to apply.

This is not just my opinion or that of a handful of observers. In 2008, a study was done on the Johnson Amendment by the Congressional Research Service. Its report stated, "The line between what is prohibited and what is permitted can be difficult to discern."[9] In fact, according to many experts, the IRS has never specified the precise standards it uses to regulate an area this sensitive. Instead of adding precision, a highly political IRS has brought vagueness by means of its various publications and documents. And these, let us remember, do not have the force of law.

As Stanley relates, after the Johnson Amendment passed, the IRS proceeded to deny tax-exempt status to so-called action organizations, those entities that involve themselves in political campaigns. The regulations specify that to determine whether an entity falls into the "action organization" category, "all the surrounding facts and circumstances, including the articles [of incorporation] and all activities of the organization, are to be considered."[10] From one point of view, this standard itself is not a standard at all, but a mere statement of the obvious. Obviously, a consideration of "all the surrounding facts and circumstances" can only happen after the action has been taken, and perhaps a long time after. The conclusion? We cannot really know whether we are about to cross the line, or whether we have crossed the line after action is taken. After all, we never know when a new fact or circumstance may come to light.

The way the "facts and circumstances" test plays out is seen in the various IRS publications, particularly Publication 1828 (aka *Tax Guide for Churches & Religious Organizations*), in which the IRS gives examples of what is or is not considered as prohibited political intervention. As Stanley points out, however, even IRS training materials admit the vagueness of the regulations: "In situations where there is no explicit endorsement or partisan activity, there is no bright-line test for determining if the 501(c)(3) organization participated or intervened in a political campaign." The Congressional Research Service report mentioned earlier also states, "In many situations, the activity is permissible unless it is structured or conducted in a way that shows bias towards or against a candidate. Some biases can be subtle and whether an activity is campaign intervention will depend on the facts and circumstances of each case."[11]

Now, here's the problem. If the teaching of the Church or the message of the Gospels corresponds to the position of one particular political party or candidate, what protects a church from the accusation of being biased or partisan?

Where things become even more complex is when we consider that churches and other tax-exempt organizations do not simply read the IRS interpretations of the IRC laws. They rely, in the end, on the advice of their attorneys. And not all legal advice is created equal. Indeed, some attorneys are highly trained in this particular area of the law. Others are moderately familiar with it. And still others are not trained in it at all. What we end up with is a wide variety of different legal opinions about an inherently vague interpretation of an already vague provision of law with questionable origins.

The Office of the General Counsel for the United States Conference of Catholic Bishops issues a document of general legal guidance on these matters every few years. That document admits unhelpfully, "General guidance cannot anticipate every conceivable fact pattern, nor can it substitute for the advice Catholic organizations should seek from their own attorneys." The solution: difficult questions "should be resolved with the advice of diocesan legal counsel. Such counsel should be sought prior to engaging in potentially problematic activities."[12]

A particular problem arises here when it comes to the institutional Catholic Church and the legal advice on which it relies. Attorneys hired by Church agencies render opinions that result in policies of the bishops' conferences and the individual dioceses and therefore trickle down to the parishes. The legal opinions on which these policies rest, to be sure, are interpretations of the IRS interpretations of the Johnson Amendment. They are, by definition, already several steps removed from the authority of law and from any certainty regarding the meaning of that law. They are no more than opinions about opinions. Yet because the policies based on those opinions come from the offices of bishops, faithful Catholics—who are rightly trained to revere and obey their bishops—easily read more dogmatic force and certainty into these policies than they deserve. In other words, the chilling effect of vague tax law is reinforced by the very institution whose activities are thereby chilled.

This would be frustrating enough if we were discussing laws about importing fruit from South America or buying cigarettes in North Carolina, but we discuss here the quintessential freedoms of our democracy. These include the right to speak out and participate in the decisions about whom we will elect to govern us and the right to proclaim the Word of God and the demands of the Gospel regarding those same decisions. Many of these are life-and-death decisions inasmuch as they affect public policy on abortion.

BE NOT AFRAID (OF THE IRS)

As Erik Stanley astutely observes, "The predictable outcome of this state of affairs has been massive self-censorship among churches and pastors."[13] Even the Supreme Court, on more than one occasion, has noted with concern what happens when people aren't given a clear, bright line regarding what speech and activity is forbidden and what is not. Said the court in *Grayned v. City of Rockford*, affirming an earlier decision: "Uncertain meanings inevitably lead citizens to 'steer far wider of the unlawful zone . . . than if the boundaries of the forbidden areas were clearly marked.'"[14]

In *Virginia v. Hicks*, the court again criticized vague boundaries: "Many persons, rather than undertake the considerable burden (and sometimes risk) of vindicating their rights through case-by-case litigation, will choose simply to abstain from protected speech—harming not only themselves but society as a whole, which is deprived of an uninhibited marketplace of ideas."[15]

Stanley rightly asks, "If legal scholars, attorneys, and even the IRS itself cannot agree—and, in fact, argue—over where the line is drawn under the Johnson Amendment, how can the IRS realistically expect pastors to understand and apply these questionable speech restrictions?"[16] The answer, of course, is that it can't. And pastors know that. So the easiest, safest route is to do nothing in the area of political speech or what may be perceived as political speech. This easy way out is made even easier when the policy of a church hierarchy essentially says, "Stay away from this."

In reality, however, there is no justification for either the fear or the chill. If the interpretation by the IRS of an already vague amendment leaves it even more vague, the actions of the agency responsible for both its interpretation and enforcement suggest a likely outcome. After all, actions speak louder than words. When we look at the enforcement history of the IRS in reference to the Johnson Amendment, we see, in fact, a whole lot of nothing. There simply is no meaningful, consistent enforcement. None of the words that can so easily scare people about the "revocation of tax-exempt status" seem to have any real teeth in practice.

Incredibly, in the sixty-year history of the Johnson Amendment, among the three hundred thousand churches in America, only one church has lost its tax-exempt status, and that just for one day. And not one has lost its tax-exempt status, even for a day, because of something that was preached in a pulpit, taught in a classroom, printed in the church bulletin, or distributed to the congregation. Pause for a moment to absorb that fact. What so many of us are afraid of—namely, that the state is going to require our church to pay large sums of taxes as a result of its political intervention—has never happened, not even once. Further still from reality is what some paint as a nationwide scenario of an entire denomination losing its tax exemption.

I once sat in a workshop about the implications of the Johnson Amendment for Catholic publications. The workshop was held at the annual convention of the Catholic Press Association and was presented by a representative of the U.S. Conference of Catholic Bishops. We heard a lengthy and detailed explanation of "do's and don'ts"—mostly "don'ts"—with a repeated emphasis on risks and, of course, on "facts and circumstances." When the Q&A session began toward the end of the workshop, I asked if any Catholic publication had ever lost its tax-exempt status due to any of the violations that we were being warned about. The answer was no.

The one case where a church had its tax exemption revoked for a single day came about when the IRS revoked its advance determination letter attesting to the exemption. As we have already pointed out, a church does not need such a letter. It can always present itself as exempt by law. The federal court case cited earlier, *Branch Ministries v. Rossotti*, affirms this truth in regard to the one church that temporarily lost its tax status. It was not a sermon that caused the problem, but rather a full-page ad urging citizens not to vote for candidate Bill Clinton. That, of course, was clearly an intervention in a political race.

We can all remember numerous examples of candidates appearing in a church, speaking and even receiving a pastor's glowing endorsement. Yet, none of these churches received the same treatment. In the *Branch Ministries* case, the church's attorney essentially asked the court why this church was being punished for "political intervention" when obviously so many other churches were doing it and getting away with it. As the court explained, the IRS could conceivably have revoked the exemptions of those other churches if they did something so publicly provocative as place a paid ad in a newspaper with an explicit appeal not to vote for a candidate. The enforcement is obviously minimal, selective, and subjective.

Despite the inconvenience, no tax was assessed to the church in question. Nor was any penalty imposed. The "loss" of exemption covered only the day the church ran the ad. The next day, everything was back to normal! Here are the actual words of the Rossotti decision regarding the impact—or lack thereof—of the judgment against the church:

> Because of the unique treatment churches receive under the Internal Revenue Code, the impact of the revocation is likely to be more symbolic than substantial. As the IRS confirmed at oral argument, if the Church does not intervene in future political campaigns, it may hold itself out as a 501(c)(3) organization and receive all the benefits of that status. All that will have been lost,

in that event, is the advance assurance of deductibility in the event a donor should be audited.[17]

Another case to consider is one involving All Saints Episcopal Church in Pasadena, California. In the Bush–Kerry presidential election, a visiting minister conducted a mock debate. "Jesus" was the moderator, and he criticized President Bush. As a result, the IRS undertook an audit of the church that went on for twenty-seven months. The church stood firmly for its freedom to speak. In the end, no penalties were imposed, despite the fact that the IRS sent a letter saying that the church did intervene in the race and should not do it again. Yet still, there was no explanation of where the boundary line was, and once again, the IRS kept itself out of a court case that might indeed have clarified that boundary more precisely.

During the 2004 election cycle, our own ministry, Priests for Life, reached a high point of activity and visibility, and this led to an IRS political audit. The IRS had recently launched an initiative called PACI, the Political Activities Compliance Initiative. For whatever reason, the agency wanted to appear tough and swift on enforcing the Johnson Amendment. But in the end, it was more bark than bite. After a couple of years, a hundred cases had been investigated, but no church had its tax-exempt status revoked. The project then seemed to fade away with no explanation as to why. The IRS also conducted an investigation into the "political activities" of Priests for Life, but again did not touch our tax-exempt status nor find any reason to impose a penalty.

All of this is meant to drive home a simple lesson. The political intervention prohibition has shaky and questionable origins and ill-defined boundaries. What is more, its enforcement history can only be described as unequal, inconsistent, and downright wimpy. What is clear too is that the IRS as an agency is not accountable to anyone for how it enforces, or does not enforce, the prohibition arising from the Johnson Amendment.

The IRS will bark at churches and organizations but almost never bite. If the IRS does launch an audit, its agents inevitably satisfy themselves with the church's promise not to commit the offending activity again, no matter how ill defined the activity. Churches and organizations that *do* stand up to the IRS get them to back off eventually because the IRS does not want its vague prohibition clarified, or struck down, in court. This is not a story of some measured, legal enforcement of a well-defined law, but rather, of a game of intimidation and power.

A court case on the part of a church—or other organization—that claims to be unfairly treated by the IRS in the matter of prohibited political intervention would force a clarification of exactly where the boundaries of the law are. Such a clarification, of course, would be in the best interests of all Americans, all churches, and all tax-exempt organizations. It would be a huge boost to the political discourse in America, which, as the Supreme Court has said, "should be uninhibited, robust, and wide-open."[18]

The IRS, however, would not necessarily see such a ruling as in its best interests. Clear guidelines would strictly limit its ability to manipulate and intimidate. The IRS is an agency that has broad and capricious enforcement power. Its administrators like exercising their own power—as we saw in the IRS intimidation of Tea Party groups before the 2012 election—and this is a power they protect by keeping themselves out of court. But in America, the law starts with the Constitution. Laws are passed in accordance with it, and government agencies must conform to those laws.

USING OUR COMMON SENSE

One good way to resolve the confusion regarding the IRS guidelines and to steady the nerves of the Church's ministers would be the adoption by the federal government of the *Buckley v. Valeo* "bright-line" test.[19] In that case, the Supreme Court made it easy for the parties to identify what speech did or did not cross the line of political intervention. They identified specific words and phrases that had to be avoided, period. That makes things much easier than an open-ended, vague guideline like, "take account of all the facts and circumstances." At least one knows if he intends to say, or actually said, specifically identified words.

If the Congress or the courts determined by the same kind of test what constitutes "political intervention," whether in a sermon or a bulletin insert or a voter's guide or any other communication, the world would breathe easier. With a clear measuring line, everyone would know *before* the communication is made whether or not it constitutes political intervention. That kind of determination would eliminate the need for endless investigations into "all the facts and circumstances" and the fears attendant to an investigation.

This is something we should all push for. In the interim, there is much that churches and other (c)(3) organizations can do without running afoul of the law. There is much we can do to clarify the confusion, resist the fear, thaw the chill on free speech, and restore the vigor of the Church's mission to defend life. One priority is to make sure we are using attorneys who are not only knowledgeable in this area of the law but who are willing to take an expansive view of the law. Attorneys need to fight vigorously for the rights of their clients to fulfill their mission and to fight against chilling governmental vagueness.

James Bopp Jr. has provided us model guidance over the years. He has argued numerous times before the Supreme Court on these issues, has won many victories, and achieved recognition as one of the top experts in the nation in this area of the law. Let me share with you an excerpt from a legal memo he prepared on behalf of Priests for Life, explaining why our activity is not political intervention. This is the kind of guidance every church and similarly situated organization should enjoy.

In the case that follows, Bopp analyzed the effect of Revenue Ruling 2004–6, the most recent guidance provided by the IRS, on the activities of Priests for Life. In that ruling, as Bopp explained, the IRS listed the following as factors that would suggest that an organization had crossed the line into outright political advocacy:

1. The communication identifies a candidate for public office;
2. The timing of the communication coincides with an electoral campaign;
3. The communication targets voters in a particular election;
4. The communication identifies that candidate's position on the public policy issue that is the subject of the communication;
5. The position of the candidate on the public policy issue has been raised as distinguishing the candidate from others in the campaign, either in the communication itself or in other public communications; and
6. The communication is not part of an ongoing series on substantially similar advocacy communications by the organization on the same issue.[20]

Instead of skirting around these directives fearfully or yielding blindly to them, Bopp addressed them head-on. Here's his response:

Priests for Life passes every part of this test: a) It does not identify candidates for public office; b) It supports the right to life all year every year, not just in election years; c) It does not target voters in a particular election, but targets the general public all the time; d) It does not identify candidate positions on abortion; e) It does not distinguish particular candidates by their views on abortion; and f) Its communications supporting the right to life are part of an ongoing series of substantially similar advocacy communications by the organization on the same issue. Thus, Priests for Life's communications supporting the right to life and encouraging people to vote pro-life are not advocacy communications under Section 527(e)(2), but are issue advocacy under Revenue Ruling 2004–6.[21]

"Telling people to 'vote pro-life' as Priests for Life has done," Bopp concluded, "without identifying particular candidates or races, and without identifying candidate positions on abortion, certainly does not rise to the level of participating in or intervening in a political campaign on behalf of or in opposition to a candidate for public office."

In other words, our attorney is saying without apology that we have registered voters, clearly and vigorously educated them that the right to life is the fundamental voting issue, and mobilized them to go to the polls, all without violating a single law.

And the IRS agreed!

The time has come, then, for pastors, priests, organizations, and institutions to rise up, cast off the shackles of self-doubt and fear, and realize that there is much more that we can say and do in the realm of politics than we have been led to believe. The IRS did not give some kind of special pass to Priests for Life. Whenever any group, aware of its rights and motivated by the urgent task at hand to abolish abortion, speaks and acts with the freedom it has under the Gospel and under the law, it can accomplish its work in freedom. Let's go forward, then, and elect public servants who know the difference between serving the public and killing the public!

SIX

Freedom of the Pulpit

HAVING OUTLINED THE REGULATORY CONFUSION AND THE pall it casts over both free speech and the urgent mission of the Church, we need now to assess the options available to succeed in spite of that confusion. Again, when I say "the Church," I am referring to the entire Body of Christ. I beg the patience of my non-Catholic readers in this chapter and the next, as most of my experience comes from working within the Catholic Church. Although its hierarchy is unique, its issues are not. I would ask readers to apply my observations, with the relevant adaptations, to their own situations.

As will become increasingly obvious, I believe that by sharing the mission and spreading our shared message, America's Christian churches in all their variety will lead the worldwide fight to abolish abortion just as they led the worldwide fight to abolish slavery.

RESISTING THE NAYSAYERS

The point here is not to turn the Church into a political mechanism. The point is to increase the freedom of the Church to speak about relevant national issues. We are not talking about preaching politics, but about preaching the Word of God as a way of illuminating politics. We have already seen that the IRS does not want to get drawn into a court case. That fear should embolden us to force the issue.

Pulpit Freedom Sunday is doing precisely that. This is an initiative launched by what was then called the Alliance Defense Fund, now the Alliance Defending Freedom, in 2008. This initiative seeks to provoke a court challenge to the Johnson Amendment by having pastors preach very explicitly about candidates and make recommendations to their congregation on how to vote. More than thirty pastors across America participated in the first Pulpit Freedom Sunday in September 2008. The number has grown every year since then. In 2009, there were eighty-three pastors; in 2010, there were a hundred. By 2011, there were more than five hundred pastors, and in 2012, the number of pastors who signed up surpassed fifteen hundred. These pastors defied the IRS interpretation of the Johnson Amendment and even sent recordings of their sermons to the IRS!

Now those Chicken Littles who run around the country fretting, "The IRS is coming, the IRS is coming," might expect to see an immediate, Draconian crackdown on those pastors who refuse to "follow the law." No doubt, they would think, these pastors have gotten their churches into hot water and risk losing the church's tax-exempt status. But no such thing has happened, in any of these years, to any of these churches. In fact, the IRS has been silent. No investigations have been launched, no tax-exempt statuses revoked. In fact, not a single warning has been issued despite the fact that activist Barry Lynn of Americans United for Separation of Church and State demanded that the IRS respond to this provocation.

There was only one peep out of the IRS when this project started, and it was an anemic one. The IRS launched an investigation into a single church in Minnesota during the first year of the project, but after an eleven-month audit it closed the investigation without any findings. And that was it. The Pulpit Freedom Sunday project will continue, and ideally lead to a court case in which the IRS is forced to adopt a more reasonable approach and specify a bright-line test that will enable individuals and groups to know whether they are or are not adhering to the tax code.

This requires, however, a will to fight. ADF, which launched this initiative, and the pastors who participate in it should be commended for showing the kind of Christian virtue that the battles of today demand, and to which the Scriptures and documents like *The Gospel of Life* call us. Yet that courage and will to fight are often exactly what is lacking, especially within the Catholic institutions of our country. Interestingly, no Catholic diocese, priest, or parish has taken part in Pulpit Freedom Sunday.

In fact, as Pulpit Freedom Sunday approached in 2008, one diocese issued a memorandum that called the Pulpit Freedom Initiative "troubling" and advised the priests of that diocese to "stay as far away from this as possible." The results of doing otherwise, the diocese warned, could be "disastrous." How unfortunate that some ecclesiastical leaders see this initiative as "troubling" rather than courageous, and as a threat to a church rather than its liberation.

I believe the response should be, "God bless our brothers in the Body of Christ who are taking up this challenge on behalf of our freedoms." We should all be shouting, "Let's get out there and fight together for the freedom of the Church and the protection of human life!" Instead, we get, "Stay as far away from this as possible." And notice the motive. No one argued that the effort might fail in its constitutional goals. Rather, we heard arguments that a priest should not "embroil his parish or the Diocese in a potential church tax inquiry/ examination by the IRS." Never mind the potential outcome. Some church leaders just don't want the fight.

We will see more examples of this attitude when we look closely at how certain bureaucrats in religious hierarchies have increased both the confusion and the chill emanating from the Johnson Amendment and its IRS interpretations.

PUSH FOR LEGISLATION

There are also possible legislative solutions that would free churches, and indeed other nonprofit organizations as well, from the chilling fog of the Johnson Amendment and its IRS interpretations. One route is the kind of legislation that has been introduced in Congress a number of times under titles such as the Houses of Worship Free Speech Restoration Act. As Congressman Walter Jones has pointed out, this bill "is not anything more or less but to return the freedom of speech to the churches should the churches and synagogues decide that they would like to talk about . . . issues of the day."[1]

This legislative goal is essentially the same as the judicial goal of the Pulpit Freedom Sunday. Again, the idea is not to advocate that churches endorse candidates. It is simply to solidify in law that it is not the government's role to control, edit, censor, or veto the contents of a sermon, or any other communication of a church. The church has to be free to preach and apply the Word of God as that church understands it, period.

An alternate legislative route being advocated by a number of legal experts would apply not only to churches but also to nonprofit organizations structured according to the 501(c)(3) framework. This approach would apply a bright-line test to the Johnson Amendment. In other words, it would put into law precisely where the "line" of prohibited political intervention is. The kind of bright-line test that such legislation would aim for, and which would be a breath of fresh air after all the confusion we have seen, is that put forth by the Supreme Court in its 1976 decision *Buckley v. Valeo*. This decision established, in regard to the Federal Election Campaign Act of 1971 (FECA), the express advocacy test. Such a test draws a bright line between advocating for or against a candidate on the one hand and advocating a position on an issue on the other.

The court said that confusion about this line "can be avoided only" when prohibitions are limited "to communications that include explicit words of advocacy of election or defeat of a candidate." The court gave examples of such words and phrases: "vote for," "elect," "support," "cast your ballot for," "Smith for Congress," "vote against," "defeat," and "reject." As opposed to all the fog and endless doubt raised by the "facts and circumstances" analysis, this decision offered a bright line of genuine clarity. If applied to religious speech, these guidelines would provide some certainty about where and how one crosses the line.

There is no good reason not to pass legislation that takes the standard that the Court applied to the Federal Election Campaign Act of 1971 and apply it to the Johnson Amendment. One of the rights guaranteed by the First Amendment, along with freedom of speech and religion, is the right to lobby our elected leaders, including the members of Congress. This is a right we should exercise.

Whichever route is taken, the judicial or the legislative, the issue is likely to end up in the courts anyway. And that could be a good thing.

DON'T GIVE UP ON THE COURTS

Fortunately, there are signs that the courts are ready to take a more favorable view to the freedom of churches in the arena of political intervention. Several recent Supreme Court decisions indicate that the Johnson Amendment is unlikely to survive constitutional scrutiny if the Supreme Court were to take up that question.

One indication comes in the 2010 decision in the landmark *Citizens United v. Federal Election Commission* case. The Supreme Court held that a corporation did indeed have the right to political speech, as well as the right to spend money on that speech, advocating the election or defeat of a candidate. The court upheld the freedom of the corporation by striking down a portion of the Bipartisan Campaign Reform Act (BCRA).

What is significant here, in reference to the Johnson Amendment, is that the court rejected in strong terms a system of complex, vague, and confusing regulations on political speech, precisely because of the chilling effect such a system would have on that speech. The court reaffirmed the importance of political speech for the health of our nation and its political process. The following quotes from the *Citizens United* decision make the point:

> Applying this standard would thus require case-by-case determinations. But archetypical political speech would be chilled in the meantime. "'First Amendment freedoms need breathing space to survive.'" We decline to adopt an interpretation that requires intricate case-by-case determinations to verify whether political speech is banned. . . .
>
> [W]hen the FEC issues advisory opinions that prohibit speech, "[m]any persons, rather than undertake the considerable burden (and sometimes risk) of vindicating their rights through case-by-case litigation, will choose simply to abstain from protected speech . . . [N]ot only [the speakers] but society as a whole . . . is deprived of an uninhibited marketplace of ideas."[2]

Another important Supreme Court case was decided in January 2012, namely, *Hosanna-Tabor Evangelical Lutheran Church & School v. EEOC.* Here, the court sided with a church in regard to its right to make employment decisions precisely inasmuch as those decisions directly affected the internal operations of the church and its mission. The court sided with the church despite arguments to the contrary that the church had to follow a "neutral law of general applicability" when it came to hiring.[3]

The significance of this is that some defend the Johnson Amendment in the same way, namely, that the church has to honor the amendment because it is neutral and applies across the board. If, however, the court recognizes a church's freedom to make its own decisions in hiring because of how these affect the church's faith and mission, how much more is this true of a sermon from the pulpit or the official teaching of the pastor on matters of faith and morality, including the subject of abortion?

Both attorneys, pastors, and lay activists should draw confidence from this recent trend of the court, that efforts to defend and advance the Church's freedom to proclaim the Word of God, even in matters related to politics, can expect strong protection.

SECOND-GUESS THE LAWYERS

Let me preface this section by repeating what I said at the outset of this book: I love the Church profoundly and respect her leaders at every level, both within the Catholic Church, to which I belong, and across the Body of Christ. As a Catholic priest, I recognize the bishops as the successors of the apostles and have always taught— and continue to teach—that the faithful owe them both respect and obedience within the bounds of their lawful authority.

Even when other groups have taken to criticizing the bishops openly, I have not joined in such activity, even if I agree with the criticism. Indeed, I have often steered others away from making such criticism. That is why you will not find the names of any bishops or dioceses in this book. Nor does anything I say derive from the slightest doubt about their commitment to the faith and the cause of life. On the contrary, it has been my conviction that no institutional body has stood more firmly for the cause of life over these decades than the Catholic bishops. Their witness has inspired me, taught me, and formed me, and continues to do so to this day. My ministry of Priests for Life continues to disseminate far and wide the statements of bishops' conferences and of individual bishops as they teach about the tragedy of abortion and call people to build the culture of life. So let nobody misunderstand either my intentions or my assertions that follow.

I have written this and the next chapter in order to articulate some profound concerns that many bishops, priests, and laity share along with me. The problems I identify here are by no means found only in Catholic institutions, but across the denominational spectrum. But as I have said, the bulk of my own experience comes from within the Catholic community. And the concerns I express here are concerns I have already shared through the proper channels behind the scenes over the span of twenty years, both in writing and in numerous meetings and attempts at meetings.

During that time, however, the problem itself has become quite a public one, and I have seen the confusion and damage it has done to the very mission, message, and reputation of the Church. In fact, it has been a matter of life and death, since this particular problem of misunderstanding and misrepresenting the law in regard to churches and elections has hindered the progress of the cause of life both in the Catholic Church and in the arena of public policy.

It is therefore out of love for the Catholic Church and for the unborn that I speak. Moreover, I believe in a Church in which, according to her own teachings, we can speak freely and maturely, as brothers and sisters in the Lord, about our mutual concerns. That is what happens in a healthy family. How much more should it happen in the Body of Christ! It is only in this context and for these motives that I have written what follows.

The law exists, the IRS interpretation is given, various legal opinions are offered, and then enter the opinions of the attorneys hired by various institutions within the Catholic Church in America, particularly by the United States Conference of Catholic Bishops (USCCB), and the individual dioceses, all 180 or so of them. Before we begin discussing how these attorneys handle the above-mentioned fog of confusion and try to apply it for the clergy and laity who are trying to live out their faith in the political arena, it would be helpful to say a word about the respective roles of these attorneys.

In the course of our advocacy for political responsibility, I have had many conversations with officials highly placed in the USCCB. Those conversations have clarified what I had already understood, namely, that the Office of the General Counsel (OGC) is not some kind of "super-lawyer" overseeing the activities of the Catholic Church and its institutions in the United States. Rather, the role and scope of this office is much narrower than many seem to believe. The OGC's client is not the dioceses or parishes, but rather the Conference of Catholic Bishops. Moreover, the OGC is a resource for the diocesan attorneys of each diocese, who are put in place by each local bishop.

Put another way, it is not the OGC that sets policy for Catholic institutions in America. Rather, in each local diocese, it is the local bishop who sets policy. In coming to his decisions, he may seek the advice of his diocesan attorney, and this is even more appropriate than seeking the advice of the OGC. But the decision remains with the bishop, not with his attorney or with the OGC. Moreover, as church officials have admitted to me, some bishops would rather say that they are making a decision because "the law" requires it rather than that they made it of their own free will. This is a problem that needs correction with a good dose of honesty and humility. As a Catholic legal expert once told me, it's easy to point to the tax guy and say, "We can't do this because he told us it's illegal, and we could lose our tax-exempt status."

One consideration to be made here is the role of the bishop. Bishops are ordained to teach faith and morals, not tax law. The presence of a legal warning does not have one ounce more legal weight or validity by virtue of the fact that the paper it is printed on bears the coat of arms of the local bishop or the title of the local diocese. The authority of the bishop does not extend to disputes regarding what is or is not the requirement of the law regarding political involvement of churches. In fact, as we have already seen, not even the authority of the IRS goes that far!

The authority of the bishop extends to what he lawfully decides will be the policy of the diocese over which he has jurisdiction. What is needed, then, is honesty. If the law provides an option the bishop does not want to take, we would all be better off if the bishop simply defended his decision not to take that option, rather than claim, "The law says I can't do that!" Now, the problem often lies primarily not with the bishops themselves but rather with those who advise them and, I believe, often scare and mislead them.

The attempt to try to make the law say more than it says, or to say something completely contrary to what it says, is harming the reputation of the Catholic Church. I have been in multiple meetings with some of the nation's top attorneys in the arena of tax law, the IRS, and the limits on what churches can do in politics. Many of these men and women are faithful Catholics themselves; others are Christians who have a deep respect for the Catholic Church. But I have heard them laugh out loud at some of the exaggerated, erroneous, and hallucinatory assertions that have been made under the signatures of bishops, chancellors, and vicars general in dioceses all over the United States. Anyone who loves the Catholic Church and/or respects the law should be concerned about this. I know I am.

That is why I have written this book—especially this chapter. To some it may seem too critical. But again, I am concerned about the mission of the Catholic Church and the ways in which that mission is being compromised today. I am also concerned about the reputation of the Catholic Church when it comes to understanding her responsibilities under the law. And above all, I am concerned about ending the holocaust of abortion and removing every obstacle to our ability to fulfill that task.

Some of the problems identified here pertain precisely to the way some Catholic bureaucrats have responded to the efforts of Priests for Life. Our direct experience with these exchanges makes us all the more capable of giving an informed analysis of how these bureaucrats are allowing a "winter chill" to hinder constructive and effective activity when it comes to politics and the right to life.

Some of the following examples are in response to particular election-related materials I have produced and activities I have initiated. As you read this, keep in mind that each time Priests for Life produces voter education material or conducts activities like get-out-the-vote drives, we consult with several attorneys among the nation's top experts in the area of tax law and political intervention. Not only do we ask their advice after submitting to them detailed plans of our activities, but we obtain a written opinion that we publish along with the printed materials and the announcements of the planned activities. In other words, we do everything humanly possible to make sure we are on solid legal ground and to give others that same assurance.

In the examples we will examine later, we see a twofold problem. First, some elements of the institutional Catholic Church in America are increasing the confusion that already surrounds the political intervention prohibition. Moreover, they are aggravating the chilling effect that this confusion has on the freedom of speech of all Americans and the freedom of all churches to proclaim the Gospel and apply its teachings to our times.

This puts the Catholic Church on a collision course with herself, because on the one hand, official documents and the charismatic leadership of popes and other prelates are lighting a fire in so many people to proclaim the truth boldly, to stand against injustice, to defend life, and to make a difference in public policy. Our own bishops have articulated inspiring and forceful teaching in landmark documents such as *Living the Gospel of Life*. Yet at the same time pronouncements, often taking on the tone of quasi-apocalyptic warnings, are issued under the signatures of bishops or their representatives. These tend to suppress the very fire that these teachings inspire and inhibit the very freedom that these teachings call for.

A second, related problem arising in the institutional Catholic Church is one raised eloquently by Russell Shaw, a former spokesman for the U.S. Conference of Catholic Bishops, in his book *Nothing to Hide: Secrecy, Communication, and Communion in the Catholic Church.* He has documented a pattern of dysfunctional communication within a closed system whose operatives do not respect groups outside of its self-defined boundaries and who often show contempt for many within it. Decisions are made without explanation, and the decision makers close themselves off to consultation and criticism. All of this is harmful to the Catholic Church's mission. To advance that mission, and to bring an end to the evil of abortion, a sincere and deep reform within these institutional structures is needed immediately.

YES, EDUCATE THE VOTERS

In 2004, the apostolate "Catholic Answers" issued a booklet called *Voter's Guide for Serious Catholics.* Although a popular tool among the Catholic faithful, the term "voter's guide" is used in a much broader way than the IRS conceives a "voter's guide." In IRS Publication 1828, we read, "Voter guides, generally, are distributed during an election campaign and provide information on how all candidates stand on various issues."[4] The guidelines then talk about the fact that such guides, if used by Churches and (c)(3) organizations, must be nonpartisan. But the Catholic Answers guide is not technically a "voter's guide" because it does not talk about specific elections or specific candidates or their positions at all. It simply talks about issues and the Catholic Church's teaching on those issues.

The very title of the booklet, however, caused many of the dioceses and Catholic conferences to reject it. They apparently assumed it fit the IRS criteria of "voter's guides" in the more technical sense. In the thinking of the IRS, however, something like the *Voter's Guide for Serious Catholics,* or like the booklet we produced at Priests for

Life called *Voting with a Clear Conscience*, would fall under the broader category of "voter education" materials. These too are supposed to be nonpartisan, and in fact, we have a detailed legal letter explaining that our material is, in fact, nonpartisan. But as we have seen, the IRS uses such a vague and cloudy set of criteria that one can never be sure where the boundary of prohibited activity lies. Here is what IRS Publication 1828 says:

> Certain activities or expenditures may not be prohibited depending on the facts and circumstances. For example, certain voter education activities (including the presentation of public forums and the publication of voter education guides) conducted in a non-partisan manner do not constitute prohibited political campaign activity. In addition, other activities intended to encourage people to participate in the electoral process, such as voter registration and get-out-the-vote drives, would not constitute prohibited political campaign activity if conducted in a non-partisan manner. On the other hand, voter education or registration activities with evidence of bias that: (a) would favor one candidate over another; (b) oppose a candidate in some manner; or (c) have the effect of favoring a candidate or group of candidates, will constitute prohibited participation or intervention.[5]

The Catholic Church clearly teaches that support for abortion contradicts the very meaning of public service and the purpose of government, and calls on public officials to defend life, especially the lives of the most vulnerable. So let's take the case of an article, a brochure, or a "voter education" pamphlet that talks only about the issues and not about any particular candidate or election. Let's say the brochure articulates a church's teaching about abortion, as found in documents such as *The Gospel of Life* and *Living the Gospel of Life*. May the church publish and distribute such a brochure? To say no to this question would mean the church cannot promote her own teaching.

Yet look again at the previous quote from the IRS. It says that "voter education" materials may not "have the effect of favoring a candidate or group of candidates." But doesn't the Catholic Church's clear teaching about the inconsistency between abortion and public service—a teaching she has every right, freedom, and duty to proclaim—certainly "have the effect of favoring" pro-life candidates?

The answer is *yes*. But the reason we can teach it is that the right and duty of a church to teach her message and to defend life has more of a claim on our attention and obedience than does the IRS interpretation of a law that is itself vague. Any church is as free to follow expert legal opinion that interprets the law in a sensible way as it is to honor the opinion of the IRS. Despite the naysayers, leaders of church institutions are free to use expert opinion to assist the fulfillment of their mission and to protect their interests as they do so.

There are two competing concepts of an attorney's role. The first is that the attorney's primary job is to keep us out of trouble. This kind of attorney will tell us all the things we should *not* do, so that we can avoid problems down the road. The second is that the attorney's role is to help us fulfill our mission. This kind of attorney will ask us what we hope to do and then provide the kind of advice and protection needed to fulfill our mission.

These are two very different concepts, the first of which inspires fear and the second of which inspires confidence. In the examples of communication from dioceses here and in the following chapter, you will see the first type of attorney in action.

CHALLENGE RESTRICTIONS RESPECTFULLY

One of the themes running through the examples you will see in the pages ahead is the restriction and discouragement of the free and open sharing of information in the Catholic Church and by the Catholic Church. I am sure that pastors of other denominations face similar bureaucratic resistance, and I trust that my experience within my church will help them negotiate their own particular pathways to freedom.

This restrictiveness is problematic on a number of levels. It elevates fear to a virtue and completely contradicts both what the Supreme Court and the First Amendment call for when they speak of an uninhibited exchange of ideas, especially relating to politics. Worse, it refutes what the Catholic Church herself calls for in regard to both the freedom of communication within the Church and her freedom to proclaim her message to society. Of particular note is what the Second Vatican Council pronounced in its *Pastoral Constitution on the Church in the Modern World* when it said, "At all times and in all places, the Church should have the true freedom to teach the faith, to proclaim its teaching about society, to carry out its task among men without hindrance, and to pass moral judgment even in matters relating to politics, whenever the fundamental rights of man or the salvation of souls requires it."[6]

In the 2004 and 2006 election cycles, the number of inquiries both to the U.S. Bishops' Conference and to the IRS increased regarding what was or was not legal for churches to do regarding political intervention. This was in no small part due to the activity of groups like Priests for Life, Catholic Answers, and other clergy, churches, and organizations whose activity we were prompting. In short, people were hearing the message, getting involved, and doing more.

Interestingly, most of the concern about these questions seems to have come from officials entrusted with responsibility for pro-life activities. The other social issues about which churches preach—justice, peace, migration, human development, poverty, and education—cause little fuss despite their political relevance.

So why, then, are the pro-life entities the ones that end up absorbing the heat? Obviously, abortion remains the flash point in the battles Christians are fighting. It remains the flash point because it causes the strongest reaction in those anti-Christians who are most fearful of our progress. That reaction, in turn, causes anxiety among those loyal to the Church who are most fearful of controversy.

The convergence of this increased activity and the increasing legal concerns has led to, as one highly placed USCCB official put it, "questions from bishops about parishes that want to use voter materials prepared by other groups." These questions then led to a policy, adopted by the administrative committee of the USCCB, "to urge parishes not to distribute voter education materials that are not authorized and distributed by the diocese, the state Catholic conference, or this Conference." One of the motives put forward for this policy was "avoiding needless legal entanglements." This is another theme that is at the heart of the problem we are examining, namely, that it is the fear of the fight that keeps us from doing what we, in fact, have the freedom to do. Chill and fear go together, and a necessary key to moving forward is to muster the will to carry out our mission.

This policy about voter education materials is the basis, then, for the subsequent, often-repeated warnings coming out of many chancery offices to restrict the kinds of materials that are used by parishes at election times. Such a policy creates numerous problems and, in fact, is self-contradictory and self-defeating when examined in the light of the nature of the Catholic Church. Not only does this policy chill protected political speech but it also chills the initiative of priests and laity alike to be active in articulating, spreading, and defending the teachings of the faith. It chills, likewise, the collaboration that parishes and their leaders are called to foster with other organizations both inside and outside the Catholic Church. It even calls into question the very nature of teaching authority within the Catholic Church.

There is a crippling vagueness to all of this. When the policy addresses "voter education materials," it's unclear whether it is talking about resources that convey the positions of specific candidates in a specific race or those that simply talk about a church's teachings on a given issue and not about specific candidates or their positions. And the bishops' own documents direct people how to vote, don't they? Consider one of the most noteworthy passages in *Living the Gospel of Life*: "We urge our fellow citizens to see beyond party politics, to analyze campaign rhetoric critically, and to choose their political leaders according to principle, not party affiliation or mere self-interest."[7] So are we not here telling people how to vote? What is the principle mentioned if not Church teaching? At the end of the day, we spend more time playing word games than protecting life.

When Catholics are told that no voter education materials may be used unless "authorized and distributed by the diocese, the state Catholic conference, or this Conference," we obviously have to stop and think carefully. *Living the Gospel of Life* was authorized (and, in fact, written) by the Bishops' Conference. Yet curiously, we will not see it mentioned in the memos we will look at here.

In fact, we will see this prohibition worded in several different ways. Sometimes it comes out in more restrictive form than the resolution that the bishops' administrative committee approved. In saying a sweeping no to everything else, some authorities will say that the only guide to be used is the bishops' 2007 document *Forming Consciences for Faithful Citizenship*, subtitled *A Call to Political Responsibility*—though this is more limiting than the resolution itself.

The inherent contradiction of thinking or saying that only one document can be used for voter education is evident when one considers that the *Faithful Citizenship* documents themselves quote from *Living the Gospel of Life*. Then, too, there is Scripture, the documents of the Second Vatican Council, papal encyclicals, and multiple magisterial documents approved by the pope and issued either directly by him or by Vatican agencies that also teach about voting. Can people no longer quote from these because they are not the *Faithful Citizenship* document? Or are these documents authorized by the USCCB and the diocese precisely because they come from a higher authority in the Church? Certainly the answer to this latter question is *yes,* unless we come to the absurd conclusion that such documents obtain their authority from a source lower on the ecclesiastical ladder.

The restrictive resolution is too problematic and sweeping. Besides the foundational documents of the Church that we have just pointed to, is it not true to say that "voter education" in the parish— just like any other kind of education or formation in the faith—takes place in numerous ways on numerous levels? What about the pastor's column in the bulletin based on the homily he preaches that weekend? How does this restriction of voter education materials to those authorized and issued by the diocese or Catholic Conference not translate into understandings like "No homilies may be given that are not approved by the USCCB or the diocese" or "No conversations may be held or phone calls made that are not authorized"? Isn't the teaching and preaching activity of a priest already authorized by his ordination? So why can't he draw from the Church's documents and his own formation and teach and preach on political responsibility? Why can't he formulate instruction for his parishioners on this issue as he does on dozens of other issues?

Again, although these disputes arise from my own experience as a Catholic priest, I know that clergy in a wide range of denominations have faced similar issues. One thing is for sure: whatever arbitrary, ever-changing, ever-vague criteria IRS agents are going to use to evaluate whether a pastor has "crossed the line" into political intervention, they will not concern themselves with the question of who authorized and distributed the material. The people who lodge complaints and the IRS agents who look into those complaints are not going to be impressed if the Catholic Conference or any large denominational hierarchy approved the voter material.

The "offended" parties are going to complain regardless. So do we let them set our agenda? We'll see next what happens when we do.

SEVEN

Proof of Passivity

"EACH INCORPORATED PARISH WOULD BE WISE TO ADOPT this or similar policy to avoid placing its tax-exempt status at risk," reads one of many memos I have seen in which some well-meaning church official unthinkingly misrepresented the risk to a church's tax-exempt status or put that status above its mission to protect the unborn.

Given what we know, it is useful to assess real-life examples like this that show what various churches and dioceses have had to say about political intervention and the lengths to which they are willing to go to avoid it. The memos from which I quote, by the way, omit names and dates and were publicly distributed within the pro-life community. They were sufficiently troubling that pro-life activists sent them to me. Moreover, many of the memos you will see were issued precisely in regard to activity that my ministry and I are engaged in, and therefore it is only appropriate that I respond. In classifying these communications, I have tried to identify the impulse that inspired them. I hope not to offend.

THE FEAR OF THE TAXMAN

One diocesan office sent out a letter to the parishes that reads in part as follows:

> The Respect Life Packets from the USCCB will be mailed out in a
> few weeks, but because the November elections are looming, and
> many pro-lifers are gearing up to support pro-life candidates, we

want to clarify what political activity is permissible in the parishes and what is not.

> The Respect Life Office has received several calls this summer about political activity in the parishes. There have been questions about whether or not parishes or parish groups . . . or Respect Life Committees are permitted to distribute voters guides put out by various pro-life organizations or the Catholic Answers Voters Guide that is being promoted by Priests for Life. The short answer is no.

And who said no? The letter explicitly lays it on the "diocesan attorney." The only voter's guide that can be distributed, he tells us, is *Faithful Citizenship.* The letter begs the faithful, "Please do *not* do anything that would jeopardize the tax-exempt status of the Church."

As we see regularly, this letter is filled with the dread that the "tax-exempt status of the Church" is at risk—a baseless dread—and then is filled with the equally baseless assertion that the only way to be safe is to refrain from using any voter materials except the one and only guide that enjoys the approval of the Church hierarchy. The letter fails to even make its own case. Is the argument that the *Faithful Citizenship* guide is the only safe material to use because the bishops endorsed it and want it distributed? Nowhere, of course, in the law or in the IRS interpretation of the law does an endorsement by Catholic bishops qualify as a line of demarcation between what may or may not endanger the tax status of the Catholic Church.

Now, if that is not the criterion that this letter claims to invoke, then it is not clear what is. The recipients are being told not to "do anything that would jeopardize the tax-exempt status of the Church." But how does one exactly carry that out? If the diocese is saying, "Just rely on our attorney," then the letter should just say so without all the unfounded dramatics. As it happens, both Catholic Answers and Priests for Life do the same in promoting our respective voter materials—rely on our attorneys' opinions. So now some of the drama about the "tax-exempt status of the Church" would seem to be removed and the only risk is that someone would be getting bad counsel.

We also see in this memo an underlying motive less about preserving the Church's tax-exempt status and more about avoiding the legal fights that may be necessary to defend the Church's right to teach and promote its own doctrine. Last chapter we saw a mention of "avoiding needless legal entanglements." This letter says, "A huge amount of time and money would need to be expended to fight a lawsuit." The fact that the letter starts with a wish for a summer that is "safe and peaceful" tells us more than the letter writer intended to reveal. For many dioceses, the urge to be peaceful overrides the will for the fight.

Another diocese put into its policy guidelines the following directives about political activity:

> Websites sponsored by the Diocese or affiliated organizations must be careful and diligent about not promoting or discrediting any political party or candidate nor providing any links to a political party or candidate. For example, a website promoting key issues for the Church, such as Right to Life and Immigration Reform, must avoid content or links that promote or discredit a particular party or candidate.
>
> It is clearly the policy of the Diocese . . . that neither it nor its employees will engage in any political activity which seeks to support or discredit any political party or candidate. Each incorporated parish would be wise to adopt this or similar policy to avoid placing its tax exempt status at risk.

Once again a diocese depicts the tax-exempt status as a fragile thing, always at risk of being lost.

As should now be obvious, sweeping generalizations like this subvert the mission of the Catholic Church or any church. How can this prohibition against "supporting" or "discrediting" a party or candidate be reconciled with a church's clearly stated obligation and divine mission? That mission has been articulated in documents like the Second Vatican Council's *Pastoral Constitution on the Church in the Modern World,* or the *Compendium of the Social Doctrine of the Church,* to pass moral judgment on matters related to politics. That mission calls on Catholics to submit to the critical light of the Gospel the positions that various political parties and candidates take on issues of consequence. *Of course* we have to support and discredit parties and candidates. The alternative is to disconnect Church teaching from real life.

THE URGE TO SAFETY

Before an election, another diocese sent to its parishes a memo that stated in part, "You should be aware that the . . . Catholic Conference is in the process of preparing a Voter Guide that will be approved by and distributed through the . . . Bishops. That is the only guide which we believe is safe to distribute or rely upon at the parish level." Frankly, it's rather far-reaching to say that *any* guide is "the only guide which . . . is safe," much less one that is still "in the process" of being prepared! The effect of these assertions is to exacerbate the fear and chill that the Supreme Court has condemned in no uncertain terms as antithetical to our constitutional rights and harmful to society.

This same memo goes on to state:

As all of you know, under Section 501(c)(3), the Catholic Church, as well as any religious organization who is recognized as a 501(c)(3) organization, is absolutely prohibited from directly or indirectly

supporting or endorsing any candidate or encouraging persons
not to vote for any candidate in any election. You are all well aware
of the consequences of violating that provision not only for your
individual parish but for Diocese itself.

With all due respect, I would certainly take issue with the assertion "as all of you know." An examination of this area of the law
shows that people, including the IRS, are not at all "well aware" of
the relevant law. And as this book has shown, it is nearly impossible
to find in the historical record any negative "consequences" for political activity—except for self-imposed irrelevance. Of what, then, are
the pastors and administrators of this diocese presumed to be "well
aware"?

We have examined the preaching mission of the Church as a
sacred arena in which both the Church and the state assert the freedom and protection that this kind of speech deserves under our
Constitution. The following example of a memo issued publicly by
another diocese shows how far the chilling effect even on preaching
can extend, and how the internal communications among the clergy
within the Church can reinforce that chill. We are needlessly tram-
pling on our own rights.

I want to bring to your attention an important matter: the need
to comply with the International Revenue Service's prohibition on
political activity in order to maintain tax-exempt status. As you
know, each of the parishes within the diocese is exempt from federal taxation under Section 501(c)(3) of the Internal Revenue Code.
To enjoy this status, parishes must refrain from certain political
activity. If a parish does engage in prohibited political activity,
then the parish could possibly lose its status as tax-exempt and be
subject to federal taxation.

Recently, one of our parishes had a close call. In June 2005, this parish received a "Tax Inquiry" from the Internal Revenue Service based on a homily at its Masses two weeks prior to the November 2004 presidential election. This homily focused on the issues of respect for human life.

The IRS initiated the Tax Inquiry following, in all probability, an anonymous report from someone attending Mass that the homily contained pro-life commentary, which constituted improper political activity. The investigation that followed was based on the IRS contention that the content of the homily jeopardized the federal exemption for the parish.

After a three-month investigation, the IRS did not disturb the parish's 501(c)(3) tax-exempt status. The IRS cautioned however that "any future violation may result in a loss of that status" and thereby subject the parish to federal taxation.

In this election year, it is imperative that parishes . . . avoid any improper political activity.

This memo mentions a "close call," but as we have seen, the evidence of the enforcement behavior of the IRS obviously shows that it's a "far call." Worse, what we see in so many of these communications is the absolute certainty that a sword is hanging over our heads by a thread and the complete uncertainty about which action will sever that thread. In the first paragraph, the memo says that churches "must refrain from certain political activity." Then the memo says, "The homily contained pro-life commentary, which constituted improper political activity." It then warns the churches to "avoid any improper political activity."

We must respectfully point out here the complete lack of clarity and specificity that these phrases contain. What is a pastor supposed to conclude from this—that pro-life sermons, as such, constitute "improper political activity"? It certainly sounds like that's what's being said. And yet as we have seen, not only is it unconstitutional for the government to prohibit, limit, or punish pro-life preaching, but it is equally unconstitutional for it to prohibit, limit, or punish any kind of preaching. What is to be said, then, of a church doing this to herself, and specifically in regard to the fundamental human rights issue of our day? Continuing the trend, we see another diocese making this assertion in its policy directives:

> Catholic organizations may educate voters about the issues. In addition, they may provide neutral educational forums or information on candidates' positions or make known the church's position on issues. Indeed, it is the church's right and obligation to make its teachings on moral ideas known, as long as these teachings do not run afoul of the rules on political activity.

To give credit where credit is due, at least this directive, unlike most, makes some assertion that there are things that, yes, we have the right and freedom to do. It even refers to "the church's right and obligation" to teach. But it's the qualification that follows that undoes the good: "as long as these teachings do not run afoul of the rules on political activity." Look at what is being said here. "Rules on political activity"—rules that originated with Lyndon B. Johnson in 1954, rules that are vague and likely unconstitutional—cancel out both the right and duty of the Church to carry out her teaching mission received from Jesus Christ, the Son of God, more than two thousand years ago. Moreover, the diocesan policy directives indicate that this is coming from the USCCB and the following caveat: "Impermissible Activity: 1) Do not even appear to endorse or oppose particular candidates for public office or political parties."

This, of course, is a completely unreasonable requirement. It is one thing to ask someone not to "endorse or oppose" particular candidates. And yet even that directive is vague and subject to constant interpretation or misinterpretation. But how then does one fulfill the command, "Do not even appear to endorse or oppose"? How something appears is not simply up to the one who is doing the communicating; it depends in large measure on the recipient.

As we have asked before, how does the Catholic Church or any church fulfill her role of prophetically and critically assessing matters related to politics without appearing to endorse or oppose candidates or political parties to whom that prophetic message applies? In proclaiming the Gospel, how does one not even appear to oppose those who attack the Gospel? How exactly do we defend the rights of the Church while not even appearing to oppose those who try to take those rights away? And how do we promote justice while not even appearing to oppose those who foster injustice?

As the Supreme Court itself has said in *Buckley v. Valeo*:

> [T]he distinction between discussion of issues and candidates and advocacy of election or defeat of candidates may often dissolve in practical application. Candidates, especially incumbents, are often intimately tied to public issues involving legislative proposals and governmental actions. Not only do candidates campaign on the basis of their positions on various public issues, but campaigns themselves generate issues of public interest. . . . In short, the supposedly clear-cut distinction between discussion, laudation, general advocacy, and solicitation puts the speaker in these circumstances *wholly at the mercy of the varied understanding of his hearers.*[1]

THE WORSHIP OF CAUTION

Another diocesan memo says, "Candidate Surveys that are non-partisan, non-biased, and discuss a wide-range of issues may be distributed, even in church-owned buildings." Putting aside the difficulties of phrases like "non-biased" and "wide-range," at least we have an acknowledgment that there are certain things that pastors can step up to the plate and do.

Unfortunately, the memo goes on to add, "However, I would recommend caution before approving anything for distribution in the parish." What is the nature of this vague and undefined "caution"? And how does one exercise it? Yet another diocese issued the following directive:

> Between now and the presidential election in November, you may have received from various organizations "Voter guides," with a request to make them available to your parishioners. *NO* such guides, including anything prepared by Priests for Life, other than a guide sent to you directly by the diocese, are to be disseminated in any way. To do so could result in the violation of a law governing the distribution of political material by the Church. If such a guide is received, it is strongly suggested that it be discarded.

We at Priests for Life were happy to be given honorable mention here, as we were in a number of other diocesan memos, but the fact is that we do not distribute "political material" understood as material that advocates for the election or defeat of a candidate. Notice the vagueness in the memo's reference to "a law," as if to say, "Yes, I heard one time about a law somewhere that said something about the distribution of political material by the Church." One would think that a memo like this would be a bit more specific about what law is being discussed and what exactly that law does or does not prohibit. If someone took the time to look into it, he would see that the "law" in question has nothing to do with whether materials are prepared "by Priests for Life" or "directly by the diocese." That is hardly the legal line of demarcation. That much, at least, is clear.

THE LEGALISTIC IMPULSE

So why, in this memo and in so many others like it, do dioceses make so much of that distinction? Their real concern seems to be not so much compliance with "the law," as it exists, but rather with exercising control over their own liabilities. Otherwise, one could simply take the approach of informing pastors about "the law" and encouraging an intelligent assessment of what materials conform to that law. And in a display of how easily we forget the various distinctions we have traced between law, IRS interpretations of law, and attorneys' interpretations of those interpretations, the following memo was issued to all priests by their diocese:

> It has been [our] practice . . . to create voting materials which are helpful to the faithful while, at the same time, in full compliance with the law. . . . In particular, I wish to call your attention to a voting brochure entitled *Voting With a Clear Conscience*, published by the organization Priests for Life. [Our] Counsel . . . clearly and strongly advises against the distribution of these brochures by churches during this election campaign. While Counsel for Priests for Life asserts an opinion that the *Voting With a Clear Conscience* brochure may be distributed by churches and other 501(c)(3) organizations, we respectfully disagree and, once again, strongly advise parishes not to distribute this brochure or any other materials other than those provided by [the state Catholic Conference].

Respectful disagreement among legal experts does not mean that someone is breaking the law. It is what it is—disagreement among legal experts. It would seem that the proper thing to do here is to back up one's opinion, not just state one's disagreement. And furthermore, this is clearly policy based on the opinion of legal counsel that differs from another opinion of at least equally qualified legal counsel. Which means what? Are we to invoke the "obedience" required by the faithful to support one side of a divided legal opinion?

Just as the Church does not identify herself with any one political party because by her nature she transcends such earthly, imperfect, and temporary alliances, she should not identify herself with a contested legal opinion about an already vague and questionable law. I would respectfully suggest that leaders of all churches draw from a wider pool of qualified legal advice on these matters.

THE FEAR OF COMPLAINT

In another diocese, a solemn-toned memorandum went out that read in part:

> With the Presidential election getting closer and the continued controversy over the issue of religion in this process a reminder is being issued to all priests and deacons to refrain from having the church involved in the partisan political process. This matter has already led to the filing of a number of complaints against Dioceses and other churches claiming violation of the requirements under Section 501(c)(3) of the International Revenue Code. In fact, the Bishops . . . have already ordered that no voting guides can be distributed in churches unless approved by the . . . Catholic Conference. The official policy of the United States Conference of Catholic Bishops is expressed in the booklet *Faithful Citizenship: A Catholic Call to Political Responsibility* that has previously been distributed to all priests.
>
> As such, please refrain from the following: . . . The passing out of voter guides or allowing anyone else from passing out voter guides on church property without having them reviewed by the chancery in advance. At the present, ALL voter guides, with the

exception of *Faithful Citizenship*, need to be removed from all churches in the diocese since they have not been approved. This is especially true regarding the voter guide published by Catholic Answers, titled *Voter's Guide for Serious Catholics*, which according to the General Counsel's Office of the USCCB does not reflect the statement of the bishops.

. . . Remember that violation of the prohibition against political activity is absolute. There is no *de minimis* exception under the law. Participation or intervention in a political campaign on behalf or in opposition to any candidate can have serious consequences in maintaining federal tax exempt status.

Now, as we have seen, "participation or intervention," whatever that might mean, actually *does not* "have serious consequences in maintaining federal tax exempt status." The enforcement of the vague interpretations of the already vague statute is, for all practical purposes, nonexistent. As far as what this memorandum says about "the filing of a number of complaints against Dioceses and other churches," one has to conclude that what bothers the diocese here is not any loss of tax exemption or even payment of penalties, but rather the complaints themselves.

The memo stifles any semblance of open communication with the outside world by calling for "ALL" voter's guides, other than one single document, to "be removed" from all churches. It would be hard to describe this as anything other than an overreaction.

THE UNEASE ABOUT COLLABORATION

"In our diocese, we are . . . asking priests to discourage and remove materials from other groups," one official wrote to his colleagues. We will see this approach in various memos. But how does this "discourage and remove" approach, which obviously stems directly from the resolution of the Administrative Committee, correspond to what the bishops have said in their *Pastoral Plan for Pro-life Activities* about the duty of dioceses to collaborate with organizations that, no doubt, would fall under the label of "outside groups," a label we will see often in these memos? Consider the language of the *Pastoral Plan*:

> This plan foresees dialogue and cooperation between the national episcopal conference and priests, deacons, religious, and lay persons, individually and collectively. We seek the collaboration of every Catholic organization in this effort.
>
> A public policy program requires well-planned and coordinated advocacy by citizens at the national, state, and local levels. Such activity is not solely the responsibility of Catholics but instead requires widespread cooperation and collaboration on the part of groups large and small, religious and secular. As U.S. citizens and religious leaders, we see a critical moral imperative for public policy efforts to ensure the protection of human life. We urge our fellow citizens to see the justice of this cause and to work with us to achieve these objectives.[2]

In the section regarding the role of state Catholic Conferences, the *Pastoral Plan* calls on them to "encourage cooperation among pro-life groups in the state." In the section titled "Diocesan Respect Life Committees," the *Pastoral Plan* calls on them to "maintain working relationships with local pro-life groups and encourage the development of local pro-life lobbying networks." Unfortunately, the memos sent out at election time set the Catholic Church on a collision course with herself, creating contradictions between various statements of Church bodies and conflicts in the minds of the people. Another diocesan memo drafted before another national election stated:

The General Counsel for the United States Conference of Catholic Bishops (USCCB) urges *extreme caution* with regard to any materials prepared by outside organizations and the Internal Revenue Service (IRS) notes that acts of outside organizations will be attributed to the churches if they either explicitly or implicitly allow the leafleting to take place.

Notice here, first of all, the blanket inclusion of "any materials." Again, no nod is given toward promoting collaboration, interaction, or the free dissemination of ideas from multiple sources.

What is most interesting about this is the coupling of the phrases "explicitly" and "implicitly." We have a good idea of what "explicitly" means: a written letter of permission, say, or a voice mail message. But "implicitly" raises all kinds of questions. Does this require a pastor to say he does not allow leafleting? What if he makes such an announcement, but the outside groups don't hear it? Does this mean a pastor has to chase the people out of the parking lot, go and remove the leaflets that have been distributed, or call the police on those who are doing the leafleting? These questions, of course, are not addressed in the memo, and the interpretation of the rather mystical "implicitly allow" is left to the pastor's imagination. And, yes, we have received calls and letters from people whose pastors have chased them out of the parking lot or even called the police on them!

Pronouncements like this from diocesan offices embolden priests to make similar pronouncements on the parish level. Consider this excerpt from a letter that one pastor sent to his parishioners in response not to something distributed in the church but to an ad run in a local newspaper by people trying to promote Catholic teaching:

Whatever their relationship to the Catholic Church, these people (and *Catholic Answers*) speak only for themselves. For over a year, in homilies and in the official faith formation and social ministries of the parish, our constant teaching emphasis has been placed on *Faithful Citizenship*. This is the official teaching document of the United States Conference of Catholic Bishops (USCCB) directed to American Catholics to help us form our consciences in regard to a number of moral questions affecting the common good of our society.[3]

This kind of statement is inherently absurd. As we have seen, one cannot claim that *Faithful Citizenship*, a document prepared by the administrative committee of the USCCB rather than by the entire body of bishops, is "the official teaching document" of the bishops, while ignoring other documents prepared by the entire body of bishops, such as the 1998 statement *Living the Gospel of Life*, from which the various versions of *Faithful Citizenship* quote.

No document of the Catholic Church stands on its own. *Faithful Citizenship*, like any other document, is meant to be read in light of related documents, and in fact, in light of fundamental documents of the Catholic Church, such as the documents of the Second Vatican Council, the Catechism of the Catholic Church, the Compendium of the Social Doctrine of the Church, encyclicals, and various pronouncements of the Vatican and the popes about political responsibility. Designating a particular document as "the official teaching document," while ignoring everything else, disserves the faithful and misrepresents the mind of the Church.

Another example of the chilling effect that results from ambiguous guidelines we learned from a right-to-life leader. He had been told by a representative of the Knights of Columbus that they, the Knights, had received a communication from the diocese that the distribution of materials on the property of the churches was not allowed and could even jeopardize the tax status of the K of C. This pro-lifer then told the K of C rep, "We could do it from the sidewalks."

Our pro-life friend summarized the response, "He warned me that I was 'walking a fine line.'"

So there it is. The most quintessential forum for the exercise of one of the most fundamental rights in America—free speech on the sidewalk—is now seen as a "fine line" between a constitutional right and something like a crime. Even if the line were fine, which it is not, our times demand the courage to walk that line instead of trembling miles away from it.

One of our pro-life supporters in another state wanted to distribute *Voting with a Clear Conscience* in her parish, but was contacted by the diocese and told that the state's Catholic Conference "does not allow distribution of this booklet." The rationale was "that chapter 3, 'Reject the Disqualified,' tells people who to vote for and therefore violates IRS rules." The chapter actually does no such thing. It simply points out that those whose views and actions contradict the very purpose of public service should not become public servants. That is a teaching of logic and morals, falling perfectly within the purview of the Catholic Church. The fact that making this point will help people connect the dots and decide that some candidates are qualified and some are not means we have informed their conscience. Again, this is what the Church is supposed to do.

The head of another Church agency responded to a communication from us about how we could better disseminate the bishops' teachings regarding voting. "Our focus . . . is to address state and federal public policy, at the direction of our board of directors, the . . . Catholic Bishops of [our state]," said the respondent. "We are not involved in electoral politics."

The phrase "we are not involved," while intended to protect this entity from any appearance of political involvement, actually says far too much. The question, of course, is who "we" are. Certainly, the Church lacks the freedom to be *not* "involved" in electoral politics. Rather, the members of the Catholic Church or any church are to be very involved in electoral politics, and they rightly expect from their leaders the encouragement to do precisely that. Yet this distinction is not made in the memo.

It is, then, with respect for and communion with Catholic Church leadership, and out of a concern for the freedom of the Church's mission, that I offer these observations. I hope that they will stimulate discussion between legal experts and leaders of all Christian churches and among the laity as well. I hope too that they will encourage an understanding and articulation of the Church's role in politics that is more consistent with her mission and with the boldness and freedom that should characterize that mission.

It is perhaps helpful here to again quote my friend Rev. John Ensor, from his book *Innocent Blood*: "God did not rescue us from sin and death to build a community of nervous chipmunks ever sniffing the air for potential danger. He sealed our lives with his own death-defying Spirit so that we might act in kind."[4] Can I get an amen?

EIGHT

Open Windows

AS SO MANY OF THE MEMOS I HAVE SEEN SUGGEST, IT SEEMS that the "opening of the windows of the Church" asked for by the Second Vatican Council is needed once again. With so much at stake, those of us in the Catholic Church, like those of us in all churches, need to come out of our cocoon of self-enclosed, self-absorbed self-sufficiency and again experience an open, robust, and free exchange of ideas.

We have seen how the vagueness of the Johnson Amendment and the IRS interpretation of it stifle free speech and subvert the Church's mission. We have also seen that instead of encouraging clearly permitted activity and defending those who engage in it, too many attorneys and bureaucrats exaggerate the risk and chill the debate. Rather than vigorously educating pastors, priests, and lay leaders on what can and cannot be done, and courageously defending our rights to carry out our mission, too many leaders do little more than discourage those who are doing something. This kind of closed-loop thinking leads to isolationism, exclusiveness, and extreme territorialism. This is not at all what the Church calls for in a communion of brothers and sisters in Christ.

DON'T SHUT THE DOOR

A phrase I see often in the official memos about election-related activities of the Catholic Church is "outside group." Left unexplained is what "outside group" means. "Outside" of what exactly? Does it mean outside the Catholic Church? Does it mean outside the Body of

Christ? Does it mean outside the controlling legal authority to which a given church subscribes? We never see the term defined, but the context of various memos gives us a clue as to the intended meaning.

A reading of the legal guidelines from the Office of the General Counsel of the U.S. Conference of Catholic Bishops would suggest it means groups that have a different legal structure than dioceses and parishes. This would include, for example, state affiliates of the National Right to Life Committee. Legally, these groups are structured differently than the Catholic dioceses and parishes. The Right to Life groups typically have an educational component [(c)(3)], a lobbying component [(c)(4)], and a political action committee. Only the materials and activities of the (c)(3) educational component, therefore, would be always and entirely legally compatible with the activities of another (c)(3) entity, like a parish.

Some official Catholic correspondence suggests that "outside group" also means a Catholic Church–related association, like Priests for Life. Yet to call Catholic apostolates like ours an "outside group" is an oxymoron. An association of priests, who by definition are coworkers of the bishops and who are incardinated into a diocese or religious order for a lifetime, cannot logically be "outside" of the Church and its structure.

In reading the communications issued by many of the dioceses, one can conclude that the most common meaning of "outside" in this oft-used phrase "outside groups" is outside the bureaucratic structures of the USCCB, of the state Catholic conference, and of the diocese, its chancery, and its offices. Other personal correspondence I have received makes it clear that "outside organizations" include "even those that are Catholic" and are contrasted with the "client" of the Office of the General Counsel, that is, the USCCB. The question "outside what?" would again appear to be answered, not outside the Church, and not outside the 501(c)(3) framework, but outside the USCCB bureaucratic structure.

None of this is to deny that these distinctions have their own significance and, in the proper context, have validity. The problem is that the distinctions are being used to accomplish too much. As a result, they undo the communion and collaboration that is supposed to be exercised within the Body of Christ. In more than a few instances, the term "outside groups" is used with a condescending attitude that says, in essence, "You and your materials are not welcome here, and we want nothing to do with you." When referring to efforts within the Body of Christ, between one diverse part of the body and the other, this hardly conveys the spirit in which Saint Paul wrote about that truth, or the warm, fraternal support and collaboration that Church documents on the international and national levels call for.

SPREAD THE WORD

One of the major disputes that has arisen over the Church's activity in election season has to do with leafleting, an American practice that is a quintessential expression of First Amendment freedom of speech and a timeless way of exchanging useful information. The pro-life movement uses this tool with great effectiveness.

In election season, candidates and advocacy groups create voter's guides and other printed material. They will then have volunteers distribute them on public sidewalks, attach them to doorknobs, or stick them on windshields of parked vehicles, including those parked in church parking lots. The volunteers who do this have heard the call of the Church to get involved in transforming society. They have understood what the Second Vatican Council meant by the "apostolate of the laity"—to which we are all called by our very baptisms. They have answered their special vocation to be in the world as witnesses to Christ. They have learned what the Church teaches about the tragic separation of faith and life, and so they refuse to worship in a corner and leave the world unchanged.

These are the people who pay attention to elections. They find out who is running and make a decision in conscience about who is the best person to exercise public office in a way that will advance God's Kingdom of justice, life, and peace. And finally, they take a practical step and attempt to inform their fellow believers by handing out literature at the place where they are most likely to find them. Then what happens? Often, the pastors throw them off the property! The very pastors who are ordained to rouse their parishioners to change the world now punish them for daring to do so! There is no reason to banish people for putting literature on cars. The attorneys who advise us at Priests for Life, who are among the nation's leading experts on what churches are allowed to do regarding elections, advised us as follows on this matter:

> [T]he distribution of campaign material by others in the church parking lot will not jeopardize the church's tax exempt status. The mere permission of distribution of campaign materials by others in the church parking lot is not regulated by the Internal Revenue Code. The Code and its regulations are designed to limit only the activities and expenditures of nonprofit organizations. Distribution of campaign materials by others outdoors, in a public parking lot, is not an activity or expenditure of the church. . . .
>
> [I]n most states there are state court decisions holding that such activity is protected by the First Amendment to the U.S. Constitution and/or the State Constitution, and therefore, the church will suffer no adverse consequences as a result of this activity. There are many cases recognizing the free speech rights of individuals and protecting speech and petitioning, reasonably exercised, in public areas, even when the property is privately owned. . . .
>
> In other words, churches not only may permit campaign statements to be distributed in their public parking lots, they cannot

prohibit such distributions because the parking lots are open to the public.[1]

Yet when I spread the word about this publicly, I hear from church officials who tell me that this advice is wrong and that the church's tax-exempt status is at risk. This is still another flash point of fear fueled by an overanxious and underinformed legal counsel. We have seen the unwillingness of the IRS to punish churches for their own activities and expenditures. How much less willing would they be to punish churches for *someone else's* activities and expenditures?

If a church wants to stop this activity, its leaders have to find a different reason than tax law. Some are afraid that political candidates who are opposed to Church teachings will leaflet a parking lot. Of course, a bit of political savvy would go a long way here. Candidates whose views are diametrically opposed to key teachings of a church are not going to see the parking lots of that church as top-priority places to put their literature. That would only serve to tell these voters whom they should *not* vote for.

One church official wrote to me, "In regard to the distribution of materials in church parking lots, our concern was that the information supplied . . . bypassed the normal channels for distributing information to parishes, namely diocesan respect life offices." In a theme we see often, this memo expresses a narrow, self-enclosed view of how communication should happen in the Church. The communication to the parishes is, according to this view, to come only through the bureaucratic channels of a diocesan office. This is a bureaucratic and myopic view. This is simply not the way a church should work and completely truncates the Church's view of herself as a multifaceted, Spirit-filled Body of Christ, with many diverse parts, all of which need one another, and a variety of Spirit-given gifts, all of which reinforce one another.

Another personal correspondence I received said, "However, it is their [the bishops'] long-standing policy that voter registration activity and other efforts to promote political responsibility among Catholics in the dioceses be conducted locally by diocesan personnel." Wow! What about the baptized faithful? Is their mission, which the Church teaches is assigned to them by the Lord Himself, now to be placed entirely in the hands only of those employed by the diocese? Again, I cast no judgment on those who write these memos, but objectively, their assertions contradict the mind of the Catholic Church as expressed in her official documents.

WORK TOGETHER

The norms for making a voter's guide legally usable by a church are not very hard to understand. I have pointed out the ambiguities and the road to resolving them, but while we have to live with the current norms, it is not impossible to make a good-faith effort within those norms. The bigger problem is that many in leadership positions refuse to collaborate on such efforts for fear of being accused of partisanship.

If the diocesan attorney, at the bishop's direction, can evaluate a particular voter's guide from another group and give advice to the diocese and the parishes as to how to use it, then why discourage the use of materials from other groups? Moreover, we have already seen the vagueness and carelessness that often categorize the use of the terms "voter's guides" or "educational material." And we have seen the problem with the term "outside groups."

But why can't a collaborative effort be made to produce something that the USCCB attorneys approve *and* that various groups can distribute enthusiastically? This would seem to be the way suggested by the exhortation to collaborate with other groups. An effort to come up with a mutually agreed-upon voter's guide could unleash a lot of energy and activity to educate and activate voters.

My own effort along these lines, however, is instructive of a deeper problem. After having done extensive work in national electoral campaigns, with much success, Priests for Life and I personally gained a pretty clear idea of the obstacles and tensions experienced, especially at the parish level, regarding the distribution of voter's guides. While the Catholic bishops were calling for active involvement in the political process, most of the Catholic institutions were not producing any voter's guides. When various organizations, including Catholic ones, would try to fill those gaps by producing legally safe guides, pastors and bishops would tell them not to distribute the guides in the churches. This anxiety was fueled, as we have seen, by unfounded legal concerns.

In the meantime, the voter's guides that were being produced by those dioceses and Catholic Conferences that took the trouble to do so were, unfortunately, either too long to be widely disseminated by leafleting, or had content that led the reader to think that all the issues were of equal importance. All of this often led to tension between churches and the groups that approached them and between believers and their own pastors. In the end, many voters were not being reached with the information that could affect an election.

So I sought the assistance of various officials to explore how we could begin to compare and contrast the goals and concerns of the Bishops' Conference with the leadership of other groups that were planning voter's guides, including our own, and perhaps lay the groundwork for creating voter's guides that both the groups and the dioceses/parishes could promote together.

Sadly, I was told that no meeting on that subject would be permitted because the view of the Conference was that its materials were sufficient. This radical self-sufficiency, the shutting of the Conference off from creative dialogue, continues to hinder progress. I had another similar experience regarding the attitude of some officials of the Bishops' Conference regarding our efforts at Priests for Life to communicate with respect life coordinators at the parish level. It boiled down to something like this: "Outside groups cannot be given access to our parish coordinators, because their ideas might not correspond to the programs and projects coming from the diocese and the Conference."

The pro-life movement enjoys a variety of projects, programs, strategies, tactics, and resources. This variety is healthy and invigorating. Hundreds of groups communicate their "program suggestions" on e-mails and websites, on Facebook and Twitter, on radio and television, and through snail mail and conferences. Moreover, the communication itself is healthy, and on many different levels. It is healthy just from the viewpoint of human knowledge and inquiry. It is healthy in the variety of strategies and insights it inspires. It is healthy in the creation of a larger international community dedicated to life. And it is healthy in the context of the Church, where the faithful are encouraged to share openly with their fellow believers as well as with their leaders whatever ideas they believe will benefit the Church and its mission.

After all, how do the bishops and their designated representatives come to the decision in the first place about what projects and programs they want to promote, if not by having open ears and open eyes and learning from the broader pro-life movement? The not-so-subtle implication of the communication I received is that these parish pro-life representatives can't handle all that, and they need to be protected from the barrage of material and the variety of information. So what's the fear all about? Again, this is evidence of what has become a system closed in on itself.

HIDE NOTHING

Russell Shaw, a former spokesman for the USCCB, wrote a fabulous book in 2008 called *Nothing to Hide: Secrecy, Communication, and Communion in the Catholic Church.* It nails the problems of the "closed system" illustrated in this book. His observations are a breath of fresh air because they flow directly from the teachings of the Catholic Church and her authentic self-understanding as a *communion.* What is the spirituality of "communion"? Shaw quotes Pope Saint John Paul II on the subject:

> While the wisdom of the law, by providing precise rules for participation, attests to the hierarchical structure of the Church and averts any temptation to arbitrariness or unjustified claims, the spirituality of communion, by prompting a trust and openness wholly in accord with the dignity and responsibility of every member of the People of God, supplies institutional reality with a soul.[2]

Key words here are *trust, openness, dignity,* and *responsibility.* As we will see in the passages that follow, drawn from many sources, the Body of Christ is rooted in the understanding that each of her members, though they have different ranks, have an equal dignity, both on a human and a supernatural level, and should acknowledge one another as equals. This means that even those who exercise authority should communicate in a spirit of openness with those over whom they have authority. In other words, the shared dignity leads to shared communication and also to shared *responsibility* in carrying out the mission of the Church. This, of course, includes the specific mission we are examining in this book, namely, to bring about a change in public policy on abortion and to secure the protection of the right to life for children in the womb.

The Second Vatican Council, in its key document on the nature of the Church, focused on this common dignity and equality in the following words:

> There is, therefore, one chosen People of God: "one Lord, one faith, one baptism" (Eph. 4:5); there is a common dignity of members deriving from their rebirth in Christ. . . . Although by Christ's will some are established as teachers, dispensers of the mysteries and pastors for the others, there remains, nevertheless, a true equality between all with regard to the dignity and to the activity which is common to all the faithful in the building up of the Body of Christ.[3]

Recognizing this equal dignity, and acting accordingly, means that in carrying out the mission of the Church, her leaders will avoid the kind of self-sufficient, closed-off attitude we have seen expressed in many of the cited communications. This attitude is a form of clericalism that says, "I know best," and that disregards the competence of the laity who, in fact, know better on many matters. Because they know better or may know better, the laity should be both allowed and encouraged to communicate to Church leaders. Here is how Shaw describes clericalism:

> I mean an elitist mindset, together with structures and patterns of behavior corresponding to it, that takes it for granted that clerics—in the Catholic context, mainly bishops and priests—are intrinsically superior to the other members of the Church and deserve automatic deference. Passivity and dependency are the laity's lot. By no means is clericalism confined to clerics themselves. The clericalist mindset is widely shared by Catholic lay people.[4]

The adoption of this clericalist mind-set by the laity brings to mind this note I received from a faithful and courageous pro-life activist who sent me her bishop's memo to the diocese regarding political intervention. The memo repeated the same erroneous and exaggerated view of the threat to the Church's tax-exempt status as we have seen previously. But skipping any consideration of what was actually being said, she said to me in her note introducing this memo, "If you haven't seen this already, you should read [our bishop's] letter about voting. [My pastor] and I have already discussed it and we (I) are (am) to be strictly obedient to our shepherd's message, in whom we trust."

Now, I'm all in favor of obedience and trust. But as I pointed out earlier, the bishops' duty is to teach faith and morals, not tax law. I'm in favor of obedience and trust in the way the Church teaches these virtues; that is, in the context of *communion.* Look, for instance, at what Pope Paul VI said about obedience and its context:

> By obedience, therefore, in the context of dialogue, we mean the exercise of authority in the full awareness of its being a service and ministry of truth and charity, and we mean the observance of canonical regulations and respect for the government of legitimate superiors in the spirit of untroubled readiness as becomes free and loving children. It is therefore, our ardent desire that the dialogue within the Church should take on new fervor, new themes and speakers, so that the holiness and vitality of the Mystical Body of Christ on earth may be increased.[5]

That "dialogue" within the Church respects the right and duty of the faithful to speak up to those in authority and to lend their expertise to the Church's mission. Few passages express it better than this one, from the Second Vatican Council:

> To [the pastors of the Church] the laity should disclose their needs and desires with that liberty and confidence which befits

children of God and brothers of Christ. By reason of the knowledge, competence or preeminence which they have the laity are empowered—indeed sometimes obliged—to manifest their opinion on those things which pertain to the good of the Church. If the occasion should arise this should be done through the institutions established by the Church for that purpose.[6]

I have emphasized here the phrase about the knowledge and competence of the laity because this includes the legal arena and specifically the area of tax law. The persuasive weight of opinion in that arena does not come from episcopal ordination, but rather from expertise in the law itself. But when we think otherwise, and give more weight to the opinion of a cleric about what will threaten the tax exemption of the Church rather than to legal experts, we fall into the type of clericalism described in this passage:

Unfortunately, pervasive and longstanding clericalism, by reducing the laity to passivity and treating as normative forms of spirituality proper to priests and religious, has given Catholicism a misleading experience of the Church. All too often the faithful feel themselves to be, not brothers and sisters joined in intimate communion and full cooperators in carrying out the Church's mission, but citizens in a rather weak monarchic or aristocratic political society, whose government lacks necessary checks and balances, and whose inefficient clerical and lay bureaucracy often is impervious to advice and criticism.[7]

The Church's mission—including that of advancing the Gospel of life in the political and legislative arena—is a mission in which clerical leaders and laity are cooperators. The laity are not to be passive observers on whom diocesan bureaucrats impose a uniformity of action and methodology. The *Pastoral Constitution on the Church in the Modern World* of the Second Vatican Council takes a much more inclusive position:

> By virtue of her mission to shed on the whole world the radiance of the Gospel message, and to unify under one Spirit all men of whatever nation, race or culture, the Church stands forth as a sign of that brotherhood which allows honest dialogue and gives it vigor.
>
> Such a mission requires in the first place that we foster within the Church herself mutual esteem, reverence and harmony, through the full recognition of lawful diversity. Thus all those who compose the one People of God, both pastors and the general faithful, can engage in dialogue with ever abounding fruitfulness. For the bonds which unite the faithful are mightier than anything dividing them. Hence, let there be unity in what is necessary; freedom in what is unsettled, and charity in any case.[8]

This is quite a different tone than what we find in the memos quoted at length by church lawyers and clerics. In 1971, the worldwide Synod of Bishops reinforced the Vatican II position on freedom and inclusiveness: "The Church recognizes everyone's right to suitable freedom of expression and thought. This includes the right of everyone to be heard in a spirit of dialogue which preserves a legitimate diversity within the Church."[9]

Robert Moynihan, who founded the magazine *Inside the Vatican* and is an astute observer of the dynamics within the Church at her highest levels, observed in his August 31, 2013, edition of *The Moynihan Letters* that "we ought generally and in principle to submit our own wills to our superiors in Christ, but we also know with equal clarity that pious obedience can become an opportunity for the abuse, and abusive control, of the piously obedient by flawed, sinful superiors." He also noted, "All of this is in the mind of Pope Francis—he said some of these things while on the airplane coming back from Brazil, in his famous press conference. He said specifically that he appreciated subordinates who spoke truth to him."[10]

So now is the time for all of us to "speak truth in the Church" and to demand our proper role in exercising our shared responsibility for the Church's mission, including in the political arena. The institutional Catholic Church—and all Christian churches—need to recognize that the choice, in the end, is not between "risk" and "no risk." There is no such thing as "no risk." The real choice is between accepting the reality of risk or remaining silent about the truth that our mission requires us to proclaim. We are to pronounce moral judgment even in matters of politics. The bishops' statements have called us to active participation. And the abortion issue is a unique emergency on the most fundamental level of defending human rights.

NINE

Collision Course

IN MANY WAYS, THE ABORTION DEBATE IN AMERICA REMAINS at an impasse. Looking at the impasse more closely, however, we see a dual collision course of ideas that is working itself out in the courts as well as in public opinion. This collision course is based on the twofold lie behind legal abortion: the first is that what is destroyed in abortion is not a child, which we will examine in this chapter. The second is that abortion carries a benefit for women, which will be discussed in the next chapter.

Each of these ideas will eventually collide with the truth. The first truth is that abortion is an act of violence as real as any other killing. The second truth is that abortion brings upon women a profound damage that nobody would wish on a daughter, niece, sister, friend, or anyone in their life. Undoing the impasse involves speeding up each collision. The truth, once shared, will dislodge false ideas and force a profound reconsideration of thought and action regarding abortion.

GETTING CONCRETE

Former U.S. Supreme Court justice Sandra Day O'Connor once famously said that the *Roe v. Wade* decision was "on a collision course with itself."[1] On the one hand, the decision gave the states the right to protect unborn children after viability while insisting on the right to abort in all cases in the first two trimesters. On the other hand, the age of viability, thanks to modern science, continues to move earlier and earlier.

Ironically, it is in the decades during which we have learned more about the unborn child than at any other time in human history that we have seen the abandonment of legal protection of that child. Yet now, a massive cognitive dissonance is developing, as medical science calls the unborn our "newest patient," as fetal therapy and surgery continue to develop, as the imaging of the unborn is perfected, and even as psychology and learning patterns of the unborn are better understood.

In the law itself, we see a new reality emerging. In the United States, for instance, federal law now protects children born alive at any stage, even as a result of a failed abortion, and protects the unborn from the specific procedure of partial-birth abortion. What is more, federal law and some state laws recognize unborn children as victims if they are killed in the commission of a crime. This leads to the curious contradiction that if a pregnant woman on her way to an abortion is struck by a drunk driver, that driver can be charged with the death of the child she was about to have legally killed.

The public is awakening to the fact that when we allow the killing of one group of human beings, we endanger all the rest. The recent trial and conviction of Philadelphia abortionist Kermit Gosnell has focused new attention on late-term abortion and on the killing of babies in abortion clinics. In the way of background, Gosnell was sentenced in 2013 to three life sentences for killing babies *outside the womb*. The Department of Health in Pennsylvania had the authority to shut down his facility and its filthy environment long before it was raided in 2010 for reasons unrelated to abortion. But before that raid, no representative of the Department of Health had visited the clinic since 1993, despite the fact that in 1996 the department was notified that a woman had suffered a perforated uterus there and that in 2002 and again in 2009 the department was notified that women had died there. None of those reports were investigated. The grand jury report in 2011 concluded, "We think the reason no one acted is because the women in question were poor and of color, because the victims were infants without identities, and because the subject was the political football of abortion."[2]

Along with various members of our Priests for Life team, I was present in the courtroom for the Gosnell trial. Never in the courtroom was there a doubt raised that these were human children and that he had killed them. The argument was all about where they were located when they were killed. The absurdity of this was profound—as if a trial were under way for a man who had killed his wife, and the sole point of the argument was whether he had killed her in their house or out on the street.

Was abortionist Kermit Gosnell crazy, or was he simply following the logic of legal abortion? After all, *Roe v. Wade* never claimed that the unborn child was not human. The justices simply declared that, whether human or not, the unborn is not a person under the law. Hence the court taught that some human beings are not necessarily human persons. Controversial "ethicist" Peter Singer said long ago, "[T]he location of the baby inside or outside the womb cannot make such a crucial moral difference,"[3] and that to be consistent, there are only two possibilities, namely, "oppose abortion, or allow infanticide."[4]

In March 2013, a Planned Parenthood lobbyist named Alisa LaPolt Snow testified at a Florida legislative hearing and was asked this question: "If a baby is born on a table as a result of a botched abortion, what would Planned Parenthood want to have happen to that child that is struggling for life?" She responded, "We believe that any decision that's made should be left up to the woman, her family, and the physician."[5]

About a year earlier, the *Journal of Medical Ethics* published an article by Alberto Giubilini and Francesca Minerva titled "After-Birth Abortion: Why Should the Baby Live?" The authors coldly state, "The moral status of an infant is equivalent to that of a fetus in the sense that both lack those properties that justify the attribution of a right to life to an individual."[6]

So when the public is horrified that Kermit Gosnell snipped the spinal cords of babies born alive, or when they are horrified that he performed abortions in the final months of pregnancy, they are not horrified by some anomaly, but by an abortion mind-set that simply exalts choice above life.

Here we learn how to begin overcoming that mind-set: bring it down from the abstract to the concrete. Show and describe the actual evidence of what abortion does, submit it to the court of public opinion, and bring it into the court of law. We are seeing progress in this arena. A law passed in South Dakota in 2005, and subsequently upheld in federal court, actually requires abortionists to tell the woman who comes for an abortion that the procedure destroys a "whole, separate, unique, living human being."[7]

Other states have likewise passed or introduced the same legislation. While considering this law, the court concluded that evidence like this, presented by the state, "suggests that the biological sense in which the embryo or fetus is whole, separate, unique and living should be clear in context to a physician, and Planned Parenthood submitted no evidence to oppose that conclusion."[8]

One of the fears that abortion advocates voiced through this process was that the state would force a doctor to convey an ideological message, like, say, pro-life. But the Eighth Circuit court pointed out that there's a difference between conveying a message and requiring the doctor to provide truthful and accurate information about the abortion. The fact that such information may lead the person to choose life over abortion does not, the Court said, make it unconstitutional to require doctors to provide such information.

We also learn a lot from the ban on the partial-birth abortion procedure, passed by the U.S. Congress, signed into law by the president, upheld by the Supreme Court, and passed also on the state level in various places. This law prohibits the procedure in which the very process of delivering the child is used as the instrument of death.

Prior to the Supreme Court's decision upholding the ban in 2007, there were various federal court trials in which abortion supporters tried to claim that the ban was unconstitutionally vague and overbroad. They argued that other abortion procedures were, in fact, so similar to the one being banned that the doctor would not know whether he had committed illegal activity or not. To make this argument, however, the abortion supporters had to have practicing abortionists testify, under oath, as to the details of these various abortion procedures, not only the partial-birth abortion, but also the D&E (dilation and evacuation) abortion, in which the infant is dismembered with the doctor's forceps and removed from the womb. In this very testimony, the public, the legislators, and the courts had the most powerful education ever about the gruesome details of abortion, and this education has led people away from unqualified support of abortion.

THE REALITY OF FETAL PAIN

As a result of this testimony, fetal pain became part of the discussion and has led to further legislative developments. Consider the following exchange that took place in 2004 in the U.S. District Court, Southern District of New York, between Judge Richard Casey and abortionist Timothy Johnson. Johnson was testifying in the case *National Abortion Federation, et. al. v. Ashcroft*, which dealt with the ban on partial-birth abortion.

> **the court:** [L]et me just ask you a couple questions,
> Dr. Johnson. I heard you talk a lot today about
> dismemberment D&E procedure, second trimester;
> does the fetus feel pain?

the witness: I guess I—

the court: There are studies, I'm told, that says they do. Is that correct? . . .

the witness: I'm aware of fetal behavioral studies that have looked at fetal responses to noxious stimuli.

the court: Does it ever cross your mind when you are doing a dismemberment?

the witness: I guess whenever I—

the court: Simple question, Doctor. Does it cross your mind?

the witness: Does the fetus having pain cross your mind?

the court: Yes.

the witness: No.

the court: Never crossed your mind.

the witness: No.[9]

While the idea of fetal pain apparently doesn't cross the abortionist's mind, it does cross the minds of legislators and the public. As of 2013, ten states had passed laws protecting unborn children from twenty weeks of development forward, based on the strong scientific consensus that by this stage the baby feels pain. And even on the federal level, the U.S. House of Representatives passed the same measure. The courts have recognized that the states have interests in protecting life in the womb, and in fact, can define for themselves what those interests are. In this case, the stated interest is to protect unborn children from pain.

Abortion advocates want abortion to have the privileged status accorded by courts to freedom of speech and freedom of religion. They insist that courts use very strict standards for constitutional review of any legislative efforts to respect unborn human life, and that if a law regulating abortion might be unconstitutional even in a rare and hypothetical circumstance, the whole law should be thrown out. In its 2007 *Gonzales* decision upholding the ban on partial-birth abortion, the U.S. Supreme Court rejected this approach.[10] The court sent the message that it will not strike down abortion regulations simply because they are abortion regulations. Nor will the courts strike down abortion laws based merely on abortion proponents' speculative claims. The court reaffirmed that states have legitimate interests in protecting fetal life and the health of women.

FORCE A COLLISION

In a June 13, 2013, press briefing, Rep. Nancy Pelosi, House Democratic leader, was asked, "What is the moral difference between what Dr. Gosnell did to a baby born alive at twenty-three weeks and aborting her moments before birth?" Pelosi refused to answer the question and chose instead to mock the reporter who asked it. Shamefully, she then took refuge in assertions about how seriously she practices her Catholic faith.

I wrote an open letter to Pelosi, asking her to stop misrepresenting the Catholic faith.[11] I requested that she answer that abortion question honestly, admitting, if necessary, that she simply does not accept what the Church teaches. Tens of thousands of others signed the letter. Pelosi responded with contempt, saying that the letter was not "intellectual" in its approach but "hysterical."[12] And in my subsequent response, I pointed out that the beginning of an intellectual approach to this discussion is to answer the simple question that started the discussion.[13] Mrs. Pelosi refuses to take that first step. So does the industry that supports abortion and the citizens who support that industry. The fact is that we all have to answer the question that was posed to Pelosi: What is the difference between killing a child just before birth or right afterward?

There is no way out of this question for the abortion industry or for any of us. Kermit Gosnell and other late-term abortionists put the ideological approval of the practice of abortion on a collision course with the normal, human antipathy toward gruesome violence. To break the impasse over abortion, we must compel the collision with all its pain, with all its attendant friction, collateral damage, and anxiety. In fact, we need to *increase* the speed and force of that collision. Although collision is inevitable, our human nature does everything it can to postpone the moment of impact, and more damage is done in the meantime.

One of the ways we force the collision is through an approach we at Priests for Life call "Is this what you mean?"[14] This project makes use of the words of the abortionists themselves. Quoting these words, we simply ask abortion supporters, including but not limited to politicians, "When you say the word *abortion*, is this what you mean?" What the abortion advocate says in response does not matter. The goal is accomplished: what he or she stands for has been revealed, both to that person and to all who listen.

The "Is this what you mean?" campaign relies on the abortionists' *own* words, obtained from medical textbooks and court testimony by practicing abortionists. It is evidence about the nature of abortion that cannot easily be contradicted given its source. Those who engage in this project, furthermore, are not being asked to debate the morality or legality of abortion, or to refute any slogans or arguments. Rather, this project seeks simply to establish the starting point. "What are we talking about when we say 'abortion'?" The whole effort is as simple as reading an abortionist's quote and asking, "Is this what you mean?" They are cornered by their own words.

At the end of 2012, Gallup polling revealed that only 27 percent of the American public believe abortion should be "generally legal" in the second trimester of pregnancy, and only 14 percent said it should be "generally legal" in the final three months of pregnancy.[15] We have already seen the momentum that exists for protecting children in the womb who can feel pain. The time is now to press hard for progress in ending abortion in the second and third trimesters of pregnancy. Yes, every abortion is wrong at every stage, and we will end all of it. But we do so by leading people from the more obvious to the less obvious. Every abortion is equally wrong from a moral point of view, but not from a pedagogical point of view. People find it easier—as the polling reflects—to acknowledge the rights of children later in pregnancy and to oppose late-term abortions.

Many of the people who oppose abortion, especially in its later stages, identify themselves as pro-choice. I recall, in particular, a friend of one of our Priests for Life staff members. This friend prided herself on being known as "pro-choice" and would never take part in any pro-life event or work for the reversal of *Roe v. Wade*. Yet when the ban on partial-birth abortion was being debated, and she saw the diagrams of that procedure, she willingly signed a petition from the National Right to Life Committee calling for the ban.

The pro-life movement usually tries to mobilize pro-life people, which, of course, it should. But we can also mobilize pro-choice people to accomplish goals that advance the pro-life cause, such as laws that would protect children in the womb during the later stages of pregnancy. In the present climate this is a feasible first step.

SACRIFICING THE GOOD

There are, of course, those who will insist that banning only some abortions is not the right approach, given that every abortion is equally wrong from a moral standpoint, and that no law can ever justify a single abortion. Some in the movement, in fact, hold that the only public policy initiatives we should support are those that protect every unborn child without exception. The movement to advance such "personhood" initiatives has been gaining more strength and attracting more attention, but that movement is not at all incompatible with more incremental measures.

First of all, the very truth of personhood, the very urgency of recognizing and protecting the personhood of every child from conception forward, starts us and keeps us on the path of protecting life. This principle is not only true, but it is also the only acceptable goal of the pro-life movement. The work of this movement is not done unless and until every life is protected absolutely and without exception. And this principle is not only the goal of the pro-life movement; it is its fuel, its soul, its daily imperative.

The incremental nature of our activities—the fact that at the present time we might pass a ban on abortions after twenty weeks but not before—is justified only as long as that limitation is not chosen by us but imposed on us by circumstances beyond our control. In other words, if I work to pass a law to protect children at twenty weeks and later, the failure to protect them earlier must be totally beyond the scope of what I can decide. As a goal, I can never decide, choose, will, or agree to make even a single abortion acceptable or legal. But if the legislative support for protecting babies before twenty weeks does not yet exist in a particular legislative body—if, in other words, the votes just aren't there—then I can support that ban precisely because I'm doing everything I can at the moment.

The very principle of personhood, in fact, prevents me from sitting back and not protecting the lives I am able to protect right now. It is not by conceding an exception to their personhood that I protect them, but precisely because I embrace their personhood. And that very conviction, that adherence to this unchangeable principle, is what keeps us going beyond our current goal to the next and to the next. All the while we seek to change the circumstances so that the steps are not so incremental. Ultimately, we move to one, irreducible, final goal of total, exception-free protection, and we get there through explicit acknowledgment that the child in the womb is just as much a person as the adult.

In U.S. constitutional history, the rights of groups that have been oppressed or exploited—African Americans, Native Americans, children, women, and workers—have eventually been vindicated. As courts heard more evidence of the harm that was done to these groups, they reversed earlier court decisions. From slavery to workers' rights to segregation to child labor laws, eventually the courts get it right. Now it is time for the "embryonic moment," the recognition that the unborn child is truly one of us and, as such, should enjoy the rights that the Constitution enables the rest of us to enjoy.

STARTING THE DEBATE

We have discussed the fact that ending abortion is going to require us to connect with the concrete reality—and humanity—of the abortion issue. Too many of us refuse to acknowledge the reality that "abortion" is more than an issue but rather an actual act of violence against a living human being. Seeing what abortion does to the baby is a crucial way to do this. It's so easy for many to say they "don't need to see," or for others to say that we're beyond this aspect of the debate. But we're *not*, and we *do* need to see it. We all do.

In one sense, we've been debating the abortion issue in America for more than forty years, and we never seem to get beyond the impasse. Yet I often say to people that the debate has not yet even begun. One reason for the perpetual stalemate is that the word *abortion* has lost practically all its meaning. What pro-life people mean when they use the word is far different from what pro-choice people mean. If two or more people are going to discuss any topic, the first order of business is to define one's terms and decide what is being discussed. Otherwise, there is no real discussion, but only an exchange of words. That empty exchange, alas, means the continuation of a violence that flourishes precisely insofar as it goes undiscussed.

One of the most important questions to ask someone in the discussion over abortion is, "Have you ever seen one?" To see an abortion is one way to remove all doubt regarding what is being discussed. It is the starting point of the discussion. The image is not the conclusion one draws about abortion but rather the evidence that compels the conclusion.

I once asked a representative of a major secular news network, "Why not show the American people what an abortion is?" He was intrigued by the question, and we had a good discussion about it. He suggested I should continue asking it, privately and publicly. I have indeed done that on a regular basis since then, insisting that America will not reject abortion until America sees abortion.

At times, we, as a movement, have succeeded in getting the reality of abortion onto secular television. The way this works best is when the image of the aborted baby is somehow an integral part of a news story. So, for instance, in its documentary on the Kermit Gosnell case, Fox News Network showed the photos of some of the babies killed by abortionist Gosnell.[16] Ask an audience whether any of them has seen any kind of surgery on television, and almost all will raise their hands. But if we ask that same audience how many have seen an abortion on those same networks, we will see nary a hand.

Yet in America abortion is among the most frequently performed surgeries, over a million each year. Some claim it is legitimate medicine and an integral part of women's health. Yet those who support legal abortion do not want the public to see what one looks like. And for reasons we will respond to later, some who oppose abortion also oppose efforts to show the images or videos of the procedure and of its victims.

GO VISUAL

In discussing the use of the visual images of abortion, the real question is not whether we like to use them or prefer to use them or believe in using them, but whether these images will work. If we study social reform movements, we find that they always exposed the injustice they were fighting, and that this was an integral key to their success.

William Wilberforce, the primary catalyst within the British Parliament in bringing about the eventual abolition of the slave trade, found his resolve to do this work through the horror he experienced upon looking over the evidence amassed against the slave trade. The activist Thomas Clarkson had visited slave ships in the port of London, taking careful notes as he went along. According to the website of the National Maritime Museum in England, "By using graphic illustrations of the cruelty inflicted by slave merchants upon their captives the abolitionists also hoped to reach a wider audience than just the educated middle class."[17]

He certainly reached Wilberforce.

As another example, the civil rights movement was galvanized when a fourteen-year-old boy, Emmett Till, was tortured and killed in Mississippi in 1955 and thrown in the Tallahatchie River. Authorities wanted to bury the body quickly, but his mother insisted on an open-casket funeral so the world could see what kind of brutality was wreaked upon her boy. Black Americans everywhere saw the mutilated corpse when the photo was carried in *Jet* magazine.[18]

Dr. Martin Luther King Jr. was guided by the philosophy he expressed in his famous "Letter from a Birmingham Jail," in which he wrote, "Like a boil that can never be cured so long as it is covered up but must be opened with all its ugliness to the natural medicines of air and light, injustice must be exposed, with all the tension its exposure creates, to the light of human conscience and the air of national opinion before it can be cured."[19]

As long as segregation was hidden under the veils of euphemism, or was discussed in words alone, it could not galvanize the opposition required to overcome it. But when the injustice of it was brought before the TV cameras of America as our black brothers and sisters were attacked with dogs, hoses, and other forms of violence, people saw the evil that words alone could not convey. The fact that the civil rights movement emerged simultaneously with the advent of national television networks was more than coincidence.

In the Library of Congress there is an exhibit of about five thousand photographs taken by Lewis Hine in the midst of another struggle for justice. He used these photographs to combat industrial exploitation of children at the start of the twentieth century. He said to those who complained, "Perhaps you are weary of child labor pictures. Well, so are the rest of us. But we propose to make you and the whole country so sick and tired of the whole business that when the time for action comes, child labor abuses will be creatures of the past." Indeed, when child labor reform was accomplished, Hine's photographic efforts were credited as the single most effective catalyst of change.[20]

Government officials have been well aware of the power of photos for social change. President Woodrow Wilson ensured that no photos of the World War I battlefield carnage ever reached the public. These same suppressed photos were later used by isolationists trying to keep the United States out of World War II. President Franklin D. Roosevelt set up a special section of Farm Security Administration to use a quarter of a million photos to sell his New Deal programs.

From June 30 through July 14, 1945, the horrors of the Nazi concentration camps were on display at the Library of Congress through a photographic exhibition called "Lest We Forget." The photos had been reproduced by the U.S. Army Signal Corps, the Associated Press, and the British Information Service.[21]

Educators understand the need to portray injustice graphically. The movie *Schindler's List*, for instance, has been used to educate the young about the Holocaust. Some have objected that such a graphic portrayal of violence may hurt children psychologically. Yet liberals who support the use of the film claim that greater weight must be given to the need to prevent such violence in the first place. In 1997, NBC aired *Schindler's List* in prime time and sparked a debate as to the appropriateness of broadcasting the movie during the so-called family hour. NBC West Coast president Don Ohlmeyer defended the decision by asserting the need to reinforce public awareness of genocide: "There was a Holocaust. . . . Millions of people died and it's not something anybody should ever forget. NBC is extremely proud of its presentation of this unique award-winning film."[22]

Similarly, in 1995, the *Los Angeles Times* reported an effort at Los Angeles's Jefferson High School to stop street violence by showing freshmen slide after slide of people being blown apart by bullets.[23] In the courtroom, photographic evidence holds a critical place. "There are no charts, no words, that can convey what these photographs can," argued prosecutor Brian Kelberg in a dispute over whether photos of the slashed murder victims could be shown to O. J. Simpson's jurors.[24] The defense had argued that the photos were too distressing and sickening and should not be shown. Charts and diagrams were suggested as an alternative. But the judge allowed the photos.

Examples abound of the use of visuals to effect social change—from the images of famines and starvation to the horrors of the Vietnam War to the slaughter of baby seals and the netting of dolphins. Activists for a variety of causes use graphic imagery to awaken the public and do so almost always without criticism. Isn't it time to summon the courage to expose the injustice we are fighting in the same way that successful social reform movements have always done?

WORK THOSE IMAGES

Visual evidence is the most trusted source of information in any discipline. It transcends language and logic and goes straight to the heart, where people are motivated to take action. Language and logic have their place, but they rarely move the masses. Few people will rally for a well-honed argument. Although a photo is just a slice of reality, if it is the right slice, it captures the distilled essence of an event in a way that nothing else can. A photo is even more powerful than a video. There is a difference between thirty images per second and one image for thirty seconds.

Priests for Life operates the website Looking Abortion in the Eye (www.Unborn.info), which displays one of the largest collections of images of aborted children. Daily we receive feedback on how these images impact the viewers. Following are three of the countless messages we have received, each an example of the three distinct kinds of response we get. The first comes from a young, pro-choice advocate persuaded to change her perspective:

> Hello, I am a sixteen-year-old female and I just finished looking at the pictures on your site and reading what actually happens during an abortion. Up until five minutes ago I was extremely pro-choice. I thought things like, "let women make their own decisions about their own bodies" and things along those lines. Because of your site, I realize that abortion is not a choice about a woman's body . . . it is the LIFE of a BABY. Never before did I realize how truly horrible and careless abortion really is. Maybe it's because I'd never seen the pictures, or read the actual descriptions of abortion. Maybe I was too afraid to know the truth. I really don't know. But within 3 minutes of viewing your website, my face was covered in tears. Those pictures just really hurt to look at. I thank you so, so much for your wonderful website. I cannot express how grateful I am that you have shown me the truth about abortion. God bless you. Thank you once again.[25]

The second class of letters comes from pro-life people who are moved to become more vocal and active:

I have always been against abortion, but until January of this year I never really spoke out against it. You see, these kind of pictures you have on your site are exactly what sparked the pro-life spirit in me.... Seeing those pictures was what I needed to open my eyes to the desperate plight of those poor innocent little sweet babes.... If those pictures can light a forest fire in my heart and soul like that, I am sure they will have that effect on other lukewarm men and women who call themselves "pro-life" but sit back and do nothing against the terrible atrocities of abortions.[26]

The third category is composed of those abortion-minded people who decide to choose life instead. One young woman wrote a letter to me stating, "Today I saw the pictures on aborted fetuses. I was appalled and disgusted. I'm 8 weeks pregnant and thought about having an abortion. NOT ANYMORE!!!"

The use of such images may be disturbing, but that does not mean such use is wrong. The fact that people get angry at the sight of these photos is a sign not of mental imbalance but of mental health. What normal human being would not be angry and disturbed at the dismemberment of a living baby? Some, of course, project their anger at us. We worry less about them than those who have no reaction at all.

Our freedom of speech is protected under the First Amendment precisely because, at times, this speech will disturb or anger people so much that they will try to silence the speaker. That's why the speaker needs protection and has it under the law. Such disturbance is part of the price we pay for freedom. People might also be disturbed, annoyed, or upset by the blaring sirens of an ambulance rushing through the neighborhood. Yet the noise serves a purpose: people's lives are at stake, and the ambulance must be given the right of way.

Still, there is an even more fundamental and troublesome question to ask, and that is, why do so many people who oppose abortion also oppose letting it be seen for what it is? Certainly, we should show these images only after preparing the audience for what they are about to see. We should also place the matter in the context of the compassionate care that the Church offers to those who are guilty of an abortion.

One of the best-known videos of abortion footage is called *Harder Truth*.[27] It comes with a manual that gives clear instructions about how to prepare the audience for viewing. People are told, for example, that they are not being asked to watch anything that they don't want to see. They are invited to avert their eyes. The video has no narration so that people do not even have to hear anything they don't want to hear. The video, incidentally, has been used with great effect in churches. Yet even with all that in place, there is still a great deal of resistance to the notion that we should expose the evil for what it is by bringing it into the light of day for the naked eye to see.

FORGET ABOUT BEING LIKED

Part of the resistance to the use of images derives from the supposed wisdom of one of those ever-ancient, ever-new heresies: we have to be liked to be successful. I have heard numerous times that we can't show graphic photos, because essentially, they will turn people against us, and then we won't be able to persuade them of our message.

On what concrete evidence is it assumed that initial anger at the messenger prevents the message from being delivered? Moreover, is it true that the viewer will always be angry at the messenger? The experience of those who consistently use these graphic images is that the message does get through whether the viewer is angry or not, and that once the image gets in the head, it is impossible to get it out.

Our Lord simply did not follow the doctrine that successful ministry requires being liked. In fact, He promised that fidelity to Him (that is, "success" in being His disciples) would guarantee persecution. It is wrong, of course, to use such a guarantee as an excuse for imprudence, insensitivity, or lack of preparation. But at the same time, it would be foolish to ignore this promise of the Lord.

Our success will depend not on whether we are liked, but rather on whether we are respected. Respect flows not from doing what the other finds pleasing but from what all recognize to be consistent, courageous, and immune from the temptation to change with the wind. In some of our prayers, when we ask to "be made worthy of the promises of Christ," we would do well to remember that one of those promises is that we will be hated on account of Him.

Consider the following from the most trusted of sources:

- "All men will hate you because of me" (Matt. 10:22 NIV).
- "Blessed are you when men hate you . . . because of the Son of Man" (Luke 6:22 NIV).
- "Blessed are those who are persecuted for righteousness' sake" (Matt. 5:10).
- "Woe unto you, when all men speak well of you, for so did their fathers to the false prophets" (Luke 6:26 KJV).
- " 'A servant is not greater than his master.' If they persecuted me, they will persecute you" (John 15:20 NIV).
- "Do you not know that friendship with the world is enmity with God? Therefore whoever wishes to be a friend of the world, makes himself an enemy of God" (James 4:4 ESV).

The use of photos of aborted children does not spring from a desire to manipulate people emotionally. It springs from a set of historical, psychological, and biblical principles. Saint Paul said to the Ephesians, "Have nothing to do with the fruitless deeds of darkness, but rather, expose them" (Eph. 5:11 NIV). Showing pictures of the victims exposes the violence of abortion. "[T]oday, in many people's consciences, the perception of its gravity has become progressively obscured," Pope Saint John Paul II wrote about abortion in *The Gospel of Life.* "Given such a grave situation, we need now more than ever to have the courage to look the truth in the eye and to call things by their proper name, without yielding to convenient compromises or to the temptation of self-deception."[28]

Facing the truth and freeing oneself from deception is, in fact, integral to what healing is all about. That is why Dr. Theresa Burke, a psychologist who founded Rachel's Vineyard, the world's largest ministry for healing after abortion, and a ministry of Priests for Life, wrote that the use of graphic images, which impelled her into the fight against abortion, has an important place in the pro-life fight.

Through her extensive experience, Burke has seen the range of reaction such images can provoke. These images disturb not just the mothers and fathers of an aborted child, but the aunts and uncles and especially the grandparents. Yes, these images can wound those who have an abortion in their family, but so do more benign images, like the sight of a pregnant woman or an ultrasound or the cry of a newborn.

Burke acknowledges that some find it easier to attack the pro-lifer who shows the image than to look within at the grief and shame those involved in an abortion bury deep within their hearts. "Those that zealously defend abortion rights often respond to graphic images like a culture of eating disordered bulimics," wrote Burke. "They simply throw up and out what they refuse to digest." That much said, Burke reminds us, "The vivid truth spoken through a photograph that can resurrect trauma can also break denial."[29]

Child psychiatrist Dr. Philip Ney, one of the world's foremost researchers on abortion, has commented to me about the impact of

the images of abortion victims on children. He pointed out the phenomenon observed in the bombing of cities during war. Children,
on first seeing the sky light up with bombs, are fascinated, as though
they are watching fireworks. They do not immediately experience
fright. That comes when they see the panicked reaction of their
parents. Likewise, what is most critical when children see abortion
images is not the image itself, but the reaction of the parents, who
can reassure the children that they are safe and explain calmly that
they are seeing bad things that others sometimes do.

Every now and then, an honest soul on the other side of the
debate reveals how dishonest it is to deny the reality of abortion.
In an April 3, 1997, *New York Times* essay titled "Pro-Choice and
Pro-Life," prominent pro-choice feminist Naomi Wolf wrote, "When
someone holds up a model of a six-month-old fetus and a pair of
surgical scissors, we say 'choice' and we lose." The previous year, in a
piece called "Our Bodies, Our Souls" appearing in *New Republic* on
October 16, 1996, Wolf was even more explicit:

> The pro-choice movement often treats with contempt the pro-lifers'
> practice of holding up to our faces their disturbing graphics. . . .
> [But] how can we charge that it is vile and repulsive for pro-lifers to
> brandish vile and repulsive images if the images are real? To insist
> that the truth is in poor taste is the very height of hypocrisy. Besides,
> if these images are often the facts of the matter, and if we then claim
> that it is offensive for pro-choice women to be confronted with
> them, then we are making the judgment that women are too inher-
> ently weak to face a truth about which they have to make a decision.
> This view is unworthy of feminism.

Now, if we can only convince some of our more squishy pro-life
friends of the truth spoken by this pro-choice advocate, we will be
halfway home.

INCREASING THE TENSION

The impasse over abortion will be broken only if we increase the discomfort and tension people experience about this subject. Already the tension is powerful, and the abortion industry is feeling it.

Many abortion clinics close for lack of physicians and other staff, and a key reason for high staff turnover is that it is simply not natural to kill people. The stress is too great. To compensate for the lack of staff, the abortion industry seeks to make abortion "training" mandatory in medical schools. The goal here is not so much to demonstrate technique, but to desensitize doctors to killing a child. The move to have non-physicians perform abortions is based on the same problem: a growing shortage of physicians willing to kill unborn children. Public unease about abortion is driving the move to chemical abortion, which is less stressful than an open procedure. Of course, it doesn't reduce the stress on the victims, but it does conveniently create some emotional distance for the killers.

Abortion practitioners publicly admit a similar emotional stress on the clinic workers who have to deal with the body parts of aborted babies. In the book *Second Trimester Abortion: Perspectives After a Decade of Experience*, in a chapter titled "Psychological Impact on Patients and Staff," the authors acknowledge that when voluntary abortion became legal, some authorities "observed an unanticipated, strong emotional reaction by the staff." Today, abortionists often leave to the nurses and the assistants the grim task of disposing of body parts, with predictable results. "Nurses found physical contact with the fetus particularly difficult," they authors continued. "It reminded them of the 'preemies' just down the hall and made them uncomfortable as they thought about their own potential future pregnancies."[30]

The lesson? While abortionists work to reduce the psychological impact of the killing, we need to make that impact visible and widespread. The more people who endure the stress, the more who will try to eliminate the source of it. Those who have been complicit in killing innocents have always found it difficult to continue to do so in the face of the graphic reality of the killing. It stands to reason, therefore, that a culture that is complacent to the killing will find it more difficult to continue to be that way in the face of the graphic reality of the killing.

As a result of careful study of the dynamics of social reform, a number of significant sectors of the pro-life movement are about to launch major initiatives to show the public, in ways that have not been done before, the photographic reality of the violence of abortion. This will impact the Church; it will challenge all priests and pastors. We are called and ordained to be prophets of justice. When the greatest injustice in our midst is exposed, we need to be ready to respond. May we respond not with a cowardice in exposing injustice, but rather with the courage to reject the fallacy that we need to be liked to be successful.

TEN

Mother and Child

IN THE NEAR FUTURE, TWO ADDITIONAL IDEAS ARE POISED TO collide: the one that abortion helps women; the other that abortion hurts the women it pretends to help. From the beginning of the drive to legalize abortion, its supporters have focused on its benefits for women—it certainly does not benefit children. As the evidence for the humanity of the child increased, the supporters have emphasized the supposed benefits for women all the more.

When the Supreme Court in its 1992 *Planned Parenthood v. Casey* decision upheld *Roe v. Wade*, the court actually said that even if Roe had been wrongly decided, so many women had come to rely on the availability of abortion that now the court could not reverse itself without undermining its own credibility. And thus the court did undermine its own credibility, and it also did so at the cost of millions more lives.

BE SILENT NO MORE

Ironically, the very voices that abortion supporters have told us to listen to for decades—the voices of women—are saying now that they regret their abortions. The worldwide emergence of the Silent No More Awareness Campaign is one of the most powerful dynamics in the pro-life movement. This campaign, an interdenominational effort sponsored by Priests for Life and Anglicans for Life, is the largest mobilization in history of those who have had their children killed by abortion. These good women and men have found forgiveness in Jesus Christ, and they now share publicly the testimony of the pain of abortion and the healing that followed.

Silent No More's goal is first of all to extend the opportunity for healing to all who have lost a child to abortion. The campaign likewise aims to raise awareness of the harm abortion does to women, and it provides those willing an opportunity to share their testimony. A tidal wave of shared experience is enveloping the globe. Its collective message is that abortion did not solve any problems but only created new ones; that abortion does not spring from freedom of choice but rather from the feeling of being cornered and coerced; that abortion did not help but hurt.

Consider for a moment the integral and powerful part that these testimonies play both in sharing the pro-life message and in sharing the faith. Jesus Christ Himself is the "testimony" of the Father as revealed in His words and actions. The apostles then testified to what they had seen and heard in Christ and told how His Spirit had transformed them. Saint Paul gave, as part of the New Testament, one of the most famous testimonies of conversion (Acts 9:26). Centuries later, Saint Augustine provided another inspiring example of God's power to change lives. Age after age, those who have been touched and changed by God give testimony to that power.

Every year, at the March for Life in Washington, DC, and at countless other events, women and men who have lost children to abortion give testimony both to the destructive power of abortion and to the even greater saving power of Christ. They proclaim how the seductive lie of "choice" did not free them, but enslaved them. They proclaim that they no longer have to hide in some dark corner, curled up on the ground, unable to raise their faces off the floor. Instead, they tell the world that they can lift up their eyes, raise their heads, and look into the light of one who saves them and sets them free.

There is nothing abortion advocates can do to stop this tidal wave of testimony. In fact, it causes a major dilemma. For decades now these advocates have been saying, "Listen to the voices of women!" Now, if they practice what they preach, they hear those women's voices repudiate the lie of abortion. Says actress and model Jennifer O'Neill, one of the campaign's national spokespersons, "Experience overrides theory."[1]

These testimonies are shared in churches, on television and radio programs, on the Internet, and at public gatherings all around the world. And they are saving lives. On one recent occasion, a woman in Canada was planning to have an abortion, but was texted by a friend at a school gathering. "You need to come here," he told her. "There are women here saying they regret their abortion. You should hear what they are saying." She heard, and she found the strength to say yes to life.

Former U.S. senator Zell Miller, once a supporter of legal abortion, wrote in his biography that one of the things that helped him embrace the pro-life position was the presence of the women of the Silent No More awareness campaign marching in Washington with their signs, "I Regret My Abortion."[2] Celebrity Kourtney Kardashian has publicly stated that she decided to continue her pregnancy with her son, Mason, based on testimony she found online.[3]

In addition to those who give testimony, there are many who regret their abortions but do not feel called to speak publicly. These individuals are nevertheless letting themselves be counted by registering anonymously with the campaign. This can be done online at IRegretMyAbortion.com. This enables organizers to calculate the phenomenon of regret and incorporate those numbers into the arguments made against abortion.

Just as we have seen the evidence of the child's humanity making its way into the courts, so we see evidence of the harm abortion does to women doing the same. The U.S. Supreme Court, in its 2007 *Gonzales v. Carhart* decision, made reference to the testimonies of the women who regret their abortions. In fact, working in conjunction with various pro-life groups, we had submitted many of these testimonies to the courts in the form of affidavits. The court wrote, "It seems unexceptionable to conclude some women come to regret their choice to abort the infant life they once created and sustained." The Court shared the consequences of that regret: "Severe depression and loss of esteem can follow." In pointing out that precise statistical evidence was not available, but that it was nevertheless relevant, the court signaled that the gathering and measuring of these testimonies, as well as the continuation of post-abortion research, is an important way to move forward in dealing with abortion.[4]

REFRAMING THE DEBATE

This collection of testimony points to an overall strategy, one that is viable for the general public, the churches, the courts, and the legislatures. What we must do is reframe the abortion debate and move it from a supposed conflict between a mother and her unborn child to a conflict between the family on one side—mother, father, grandparents, and children together—and an unscrupulous, unregulated abortion industry on the other.

To understand the importance of this reframing, let's take a step back and consider the American public's attitude toward abortion. Sometimes we hear that surveys consistently show that "most Americans are pro-choice and want to keep abortion legal." The statement is meaningless unless the term "pro-choice" is defined and the parameters of legality are known. There have been any number of legitimate surveys over the years. The results have shifted little: since 1973, public opinion on the issue has remained fairly constant and significantly conflicted. As confirmed again by the highly reputable 2010 General Social Survey (GSS), approximately 20 percent of the public is opposed to abortion in any circumstance whatsoever, and another 20 percent thinks abortion should be legal in all circumstances. Most of the remaining 60 percent say abortion should be legal only in cases of rape, incest, or danger to the mother's life, with a somewhat smaller number saying it should only be legal to save the mother's life. The other two positions are that it should be legal for any reason but not after the first three months of pregnancy, and that it should be legal for any reason but not after the first six months of pregnancy.[5]

According to the Alan Guttmacher Institute, abortions in cases of rape or incest account for about 1 percent of the total.[6] By the testimony of many medical experts, furthermore, abortion is never necessary to save a mother's life. The conclusion, then, is that most Americans oppose close to 99 percent of the abortions taking place, while the current policy on abortion—available through all nine months—has never reached majority support among the general public.

We have likewise seen for many years another rather stable pattern, namely, that among the majority of Americans who would oppose most abortions but permit some, there is a growing number of those who are willing to admit that the abortions they would consider justified are the killing of human beings. In a 1989 *Los Angeles Times* poll, 57 percent called abortion "murder," including one-fourth of those who also said they "generally favored abortion."[7] In 1998, a CBS/*New York Times* poll indicated that some 50 percent of the respondents were willing to call abortion "murder," yet one-third of those people said it is sometimes the best course of action for the woman to take.[8]

What is going on here? Why are there so many abortions when most people oppose them and even admit that they are, in fact, murder? First of all, people know on some level that abortion kills a baby. Many also believe the message from the abortion-rights side that sometimes abortion benefits women and that these women should not be deprived of the benefit. Having accepted both messages, the majority of Americans belong to the "conflicted middle."

Where this group ultimately goes is where America will ultimately go on abortion. The conflicted see a need to balance the good of the unborn child against the good of the mother. They know abortion is bad for the babies, but they think it is somehow good for the mothers. They consider it pro-woman to support legal abortion. Therefore, pro-life groups engage in the multifaceted task of showing that abortion is never truly necessary, that it is worse than the alternatives, and that services do exist to take care of the mother and child.

The other phenomenon at work is denial—a denial fueled by pain and sustained by fear. Those who participate in an abortion decision—and there are more each day—are rarely eager to get involved in an effort to expose the process they just went through. In fact, the wound of abortion is severe enough that many who went through it don't even want to hear the word *abortion*, let alone to explore its ramifications. This indicates another reason why the mission of healing is so urgent. The more women who have had abortions we help heal, the more they will be able to face abortion and therefore fight it. This is why Pope Saint John Paul II wrote in *The Gospel of Life* that those who are healed after abortion can become among the most eloquent defenders of everyone's right to life.

There is an even larger number of people, however, whose pain over abortion comes not from direct personal involvement but from a failure to act. "When people know enough to realize that to learn a little more will involve some risk," a wise person once said, "it is amazing to see how little they want to learn." People know abortion is happening, but also realize that if they look at it too directly, they will not be able to live at peace with themselves unless they start to do something to stop it.

At the same time, they know that if they work to check the

abortion industry, there will be a price to pay. They may lose friends or face opposition. They don't want to make the sacrifice necessary to confront injustice. Or, more simply, they don't want to become an enemy to their sister, cousin, daughter, niece, aunt, mother, or friend who had an abortion, or who may one day have an abortion. Many people think that to oppose abortion means opposing those who have abortions, and they don't want to ruin these important relationships in their lives. For some, the solution to this problem is to ignore it altogether. Denial protects them from the pain of taking a stand. When someone talks to them about the subject, they react much as they would if someone coughed on them. They feel invaded, exposed, and vulnerable.

PROTECTION FOR BOTH WOMEN AND CHILDREN

Given the attitudes people have about abortion, and the dominant images they have of the pro-life effort, we can begin to trace several themes we need to communicate as we advance this cause. For starters, people need to know that we are on their side. A discussion of abortion, whether in private or public, should acknowledge the pain that most of us feel about it, whether we describe ourselves as pro-life or not. The psychological attitude to take and to convey is, "You are not my enemy. We are in this painful situation together and need to help each other out of it." We should deal with the individual who may react angrily to the mention of abortion much as we would a person who is afflicted by personal disasters. These are not enemies. They are people in pain.

We need to convince the unconvinced that to be pro-life is to be pro-woman. The difference between "pro-life" and "pro-choice" is not that pro-lifers love the baby and pro-choicers love the woman. The difference is that the pro-choice message says you can separate the two, and the pro-life message says you cannot. Our opponents criticize us as "fetus-lovers" who are insensitive to women and indifferent to children. But one cannot, and pro-lifers do not, love the child without loving the mother. Abortion defenders claim they are loving women, even as they admit they are killing their children. But one cannot love the woman without loving the child. Nor can one harm the child without harming the mother.

To be pro-life is to be pro-human—pro-child and pro-woman. Pro-woman is not a marketing slogan but our fundamental message. The challenge the pro-life movement gives to society is, "Why can't we love them both?" Many who think abortion is wrong do nothing for fear of denying rights to the woman. But the authentic pro-life message is a message of equality. It is a challenge to *expand* the circle of our love, welcome, and protection. This insight helps resolve the conflict of the "conflicted middle" who see the evil of abortion but think it benefits women.

Pope Saint John Paul II described the pro-life message as "that of radical solidarity with the woman." As he wrote in *Crossing the Threshold of Hope*, "[I]n firmly rejecting pro choice it is necessary to become courageously pro woman, promoting a choice that is truly in favor of women." He called this "the only honest stance."[9] Likewise, in *The Gospel of Life*, the pope called for a "new feminism" whose purpose is "to acknowledge and affirm the true genius of women in every aspect of the life of society, and overcome all discrimination, violence, and exploitation."[10]

Standing up for women is a task for everyone, women and men alike. The basis of our solidarity with women, as well as with unborn children, is our common humanity, not our gender. Whenever someone speaks up for the equal dignity of the unborn child, that person is advancing the status of women. Whenever someone reveals the horror of abortion, he or she is counteracting the exploitation of women, so many of whom are deceived into thinking that abortion is no horror at all. Whenever the pro-life message is advanced, women are ennobled.

People need to know that to oppose abortion does not mean to oppose those who have had one. A feature of the pro-woman theme is the healing and forgiveness the Church offers and the receptivity of the pro-life movement to those who have been involved in abortion. In most of my homilies on this topic, I mention the real case of a woman who had twenty-four abortions, and I proclaim that even for her the doors of the Church are open!

The Church has the perfect spiritual and psychological balance necessary for those who have been involved in an abortion. The last thing such a person needs to hear is, "What you did is no big deal." The nature of post-abortion grief is that the individual involved in the abortion has begun to realize precisely what a big deal it was. Now this person needs someone to tell her that she should not feel silly for feeling sad, that there is indeed reason for the grief in her heart, and that what her heart is telling her is true: her child was killed. A great disservice was done both to her and her child when someone convinced her that the abortion would be "no big deal." Accepting that line was a major act of denial. Healing can begin when she breaks out of denial and calls the evil what it is. The clear teaching of the Church about abortion helps her do this.

At the same time, the other line she does not need to hear is, "You are rejected; there is no hope." As she realizes the evil that has occurred, she will be tempted to say this to herself. The Church, however, contradicts that despair with the clear message of forgiveness. The Church welcomes all who have been involved in abortion—whether the mother, father, grandparents, or even the abortion provider—to the forgiveness and healing Christ offers.

Those in the pain of abortion are not helped by silence. Some pastors refrain from preaching about abortion out of the sincere desire to not hurt women who have had abortions. Yet that silence does not interpret itself. The person grieving over abortion can infer from our silence that we do not know her pain, or that we do not care, or that there is no hope. None of this is true. With clear and compassionate messages, pastors can break through the silence that led a woman to this disastrous choice in the first place.

When those in the "conflicted middle" realize that pro-lifers embrace those who might have abortions and who have had them already, they will feel free to become part of that movement. Hence, the message and the movement now become one of solidarity with the baby and the mom and dad. The movement opposes only what destroys all of them, namely, a dangerous and unscrupulous abortion industry that sells a destructive product.

UNDERSTANDING THE INDUSTRY

The pro-woman, pro-child perspective shapes both the way we talk about the issue of abortion and the strategy we use in crafting legislation. Laws that require informed consent, parental involvement, waiting periods, and clinic oversight advance this perspective in that they protect the interests of the mother and indeed the family and point out the ways that the abortion industry threatens those interests.

At the heart of this approach is the question of whether abortion is medicine at all. Dr. Philip Ney points out that the practice of good medicine entails performing only those procedures that are indicated, beneficial, free of harm, and the last resort. Ney mentions six other criteria and then goes on to observe, "The current practice of abortion meets none of these criteria. It is bad medicine or more accurately is not medicine." He sums up the case against abortion as medicine: "Women choosing to have an abortion are not patients because: pregnancy is not an illness, their choice is not an indication for treatment, their distress is not a disease."[11]

The way court decisions such as *Roe v. Wade* portray abortion as inherently a medical decision made between the woman and her physician is completely devoid of reality. In fact, the woman's physician has nothing to do with the decision. The reasons for an abortion are almost never medical, and the abortion clinics, shockingly free of regulation, treat women in abusive ways.

As I always say, you can't virtuously practice vice. If your conscience is so seared that you can justify running a child-killing operation, then you can justify falsifying medical records, committing financial improprieties, failing to sterilize equipment, allowing unsanitary conditions, engaging in sexual abuse of patients, and much more. We have been pointing out these abuses for decades, and the recent trial of abortionist Kermit Gosnell brought these abuses to the public's attention. On display in the courtroom were the filthy curettes, the dirty oxygen mask, and the ultrasound equipment so outdated that medical technicians brought into the courtroom did not know how to use it.

The Gosnell case has bolstered our efforts on several fronts. For one, it validated our efforts to have existing clinic regulation laws enforced. In this case, no official from the state had set foot in his clinic for seventeen years. Abuses could have been stopped much sooner if these officials had done their job. In numerous other cases, we have had abortion clinics closed and abortionists put in jail by teaching people—including clinic workers themselves—how to look for the signs of illegal activity, report it to the medical boards and state health departments, and demand enforcement of existing laws. Abortion may be legal, but malpractice is not. Nor are countless other abuses.

Second, the Gosnell case bolstered our drive to enact clinic regulation laws where laws do not now exist. Even people who consider themselves pro-choice presume that there is emergency medical equipment on hand in abortion clinics, that those who administer anesthesia are qualified, and that an abortion is performed only when the woman is actually pregnant. Yet these presumptions are contradicted regularly by the cases we uncover.

Third, by highlighting the damage that abortion itself does and the additional damage caused by an unregulated industry, we as a ministry have been making the case for a *recall*, as in when a company or the government calls back a product or service that has proven harmful or dangerous. Our executive director, Janet Morana, has built this case in her recent book, *Recall Abortion: Ending the Abortion Industry's Exploitation of Women*.[12] Many citizens are urging the government, through the petition at RecallAbortion.com, to recall abortion based on the evidence of the harm it does. This is the kind of grassroots activity needed now more than ever to break the stalemate.

We have also intensified the effort to call on clinic workers to be whistle-blowers. The Gosnell case showed that the abortionist is not the only one who can go to prison. Several of his employees did as well because of their cooperation in the wrongdoing. We point out to clinic workers that they each have a choice to be either a witness or a defendant. More are coming forward to reveal the illegal activity going on in their clinics, and they are motivated by the need to protect themselves.

Every abortion prevented means slowing the cash flow to the abortion industry. Our movement needs to learn more about the business of abortion to make it harder for that business to operate profitably. This helps us understand the dynamics of this battle better than if we see abortion simply as an ideology or a philosophy or a constitutional problem. As my friend and colleague Mark Crutcher has explained at length, abortion continues because of supply (abortion facilities and abortionists), demand (those seeking an abortion), and license (laws permitting abortion). We don't end abortion by fighting the industry only at its strong points (the law, media, political strength). We end it by taking the fight to its weakest point; that is, the arena of supply.

In this regard, more and more people are leaving the abortion industry because they are converting to the pro-life cause. On a regular basis, I conduct healing retreats for former abortionists and clinic workers who have become pro-life and are seeking the healing of the Lord. There is a specific protocol for the psychological and spiritual healing of such people, and they have even formed an international association called the Society of Centurions. This name comes from the fact that the Roman centurion at the cross of Jesus repented upon His death. "Surely, this was an innocent man!" (Luke 23:47, paraphrased). Similarly, these former abortion workers, who made a living by killing children, have said, "Surely, these are innocent lives, and we are sorry."

The flow of conversions is in the direction of death to life. There is no organization of former pregnancy resource center directors who have repented of saving babies and are now pro-abortion. There may not even be a single person who has made that change. It just doesn't happen. People don't get tired of saving lives; they do get tired of ending them.

Indeed, we should be inspired by a vision to which we are moving closer each day. Through the Silent No More awareness campaign, we have women sharing their testimonies of pain and healing after abortion. These are powerful to watch. But even more powerful is when the man joins her, publicly repenting of his failure to protect both her and her child. We also have the child's grandparents coming for healing, repenting of having pressured their daughter to abort. Imagine them joining the baby's mom and dad, together repenting and giving witness. And then we can bring along with them the friend of that mom and dad, repenting of his or her failure to give them the hope and strength to choose life. And finally, imagine joining all of these repentant individuals at a podium or on a stage, the former abortionist, the centurion, expressing his or her repentance for having brought to that family the single most devastating wound it can receive, the abortion of its youngest, weakest member.

This is the vision of the family, the sanctuary of life, united in life-giving repentance and life-giving witness to the Lord of life. Let us commit ourselves to making this vision a reality, in a new culture of life!

IT'S TIME TO EVANGELIZE

After summarizing the work he and his colleagues did to launch the abortion industry, Dr. Bernard Nathanson has said to church leaders, "We would never have gotten away with what we did if you had been united, purposeful, and strong." The pro-abortion forces still know that the biggest obstacle in their way is the Church of Jesus Christ. Only the Church has the divine guarantee that it will conquer the culture of death.

Those who attend church regularly are statistically the most likely to be pro-life and the most likely to be pro-life activists. Within America's Christian churches there are people enough and resources enough to end abortion, armed as the pro-life movement is with the supernatural gifts of truth and grace. It is clear that the full activation of the Church is a critical step for ending abortion. This does not primarily mean creating new structures. It simply means infusing the existing structure with greater vigor and effectiveness.

That is precisely the mission of Priests for Life. By working within the structures of the Church to strengthen the Christian response to abortion and euthanasia, Priests for Life has activated both the clergy and those who want to support them. This association has articulated not only a pro-life strategy but a pro-life spirituality.

The pro-life movement is not primarily a response to *Roe v. Wade*. It is a response to Jesus Christ. His teachings not only show us *why* we are to be pro-life but also show us *how.* They give us the virtues we need to have in doing this work. Activists around the world are studying this spirituality and making public profession of promises to live it as *missionaries of the Gospel of life*. By living this spirituality, the faithful keep their pro-life activism rooted in their faith and allow their faith to invigorate their pro-life activism.[13]

The Church in our day has put much emphasis on the theme of "new evangelization," which means a renewed commitment to proclaim the unchanging Gospel to a world that is now forgetting what it once knew. When a society forgets the Creator, the creature becomes unintelligible. The culture of death is precisely a sign that new evangelization is needed. New evangelization includes, at its core, the proclamation of the sanctity of life.

The Gospel of Christ is the Gospel of life. The good news of the redemption of the human person in Christ is news about how He unites our human nature with His Divine Nature. The Gospel is precisely about the exaltation of human dignity in Christ. In proclaiming the hope that Christ offers humanity, namely, that He will seat us with Him on His throne, the Church cannot then ignore the phenomenon by which that same humanity is thrown in the garbage. Were she to do that, her very proclamation of the Gospel would be compromised and rendered unpersuasive.

To this end, one of the concrete proposals that I have presented within the Church is the observance of an annual Day of the Unborn Child. This, in fact, already occurs in a number of countries, particularly in Latin America. In these places, March 25 is observed because that is the day on which the Virgin Mary received the annunciation that she would be the mother of Christ and conceived Him in her womb. The observance of such a day on a worldwide scale would be a sign and stimulus to the Church's commitment to the unborn child and of the fact that such a commitment is rooted in the very essence of the faith.

The Church is the only institution that has a divine guarantee that it will prevail over the culture of death. "The gates of hell shall not prevail against it," the Lord Himself said (Matt. 16:18 KJV). Now, gates do not run out on the battlefield to attack the enemy. Rather, they stand still and defend the city against the enemy attacking it. To say that the gates of hell will not prevail against the Church is to say that it is the Church that takes the offensive and storms the gates of hell to win ground for Jesus Christ. Those gates of hell cannot withstand the power of heaven. The gates of death fall in the presence of eternal life. Sin melts in the presence of saving grace. Falsehood collapses in the presence of living truth. These are the tools with which Christ has equipped His Church.

Ultimately, the end of abortion will not require the mobilization of millions of people, but rather relatively small numbers of people willing to take great risks. Consider the difference in numbers between the Founders of America and its population today. The Founders, a small band, risked everything. They recognized the principles that were at the very foundation of their liberty, and it made sense to them to pledge their lives, their fortunes, and their sacred honor in defense of those principles.

And so it is for us to do now for our unborn brothers and sisters. Let us show the world who Jesus is, the Lord of life, the King of salvation.

ELEVEN

A Foundation of Love

THE PRO-LIFE MOVEMENT IS A MOVEMENT OF LOVE. IF IT WERE not, then it would be nothing. But because it is, nothing can stop it, for "love is strong as death" (Song 8:6). Love, obviously, is both tender and tough. It consoles and it also upsets.

To move forward, to marshal all its forces, and to persuade the world of its position, the pro-life movement needs to avoid making love "one of many options" or simply one of many tools in its toolbox. Love is the foundation and inescapable condition of *everything* the pro-life movement does, whether that activity is perceived as "loving" or "harsh." Some of my good friends and colleagues in this movement say that the pregnancy center movement, for instance, is the "loving arm" or the "compassionate arm" or the "service arm" of the pro-life movement. These centers certainly convey all of those beautiful realities.

Yet the person praying in front of an abortion clinic or showing a graphic sign of an aborted baby on a street corner is also doing so out of love and compassion for the baby, her mom and dad, and the whole community. It is likewise love, compassion, and service that fuel the efforts of the person who defends the pro-life position in a hostile legislative hearing or who pounds the pavement in the weeks leading up to an election, distributing fliers to his fellow citizens. Love, compassion, and service are also manifested in the rebuke that church leaders sometimes give to erring politicians, and in the efforts of the prosecutor to protect people from an unscrupulous abortionist by putting him in jail.

THIS IS MY BODY

This is a movement of authentic love because it is capable of uniting what might seem to be divergent dynamics. We have to reveal to the world in more visual ways who the baby is and what abortion does to the baby. Our movement will make progress inasmuch as we show that what harms the baby harms the mother too, and that we advance through the testimonies of the women who have had abortions.

These are not contradictory at all. Yes, people "know" that a pregnant woman is carrying a "baby," but there are different levels of knowing, and when an ultrasound reveals a baby's movements, or a photo of an abortion victim reveals her broken body, we often hear people exclaim, "Look! It's a baby!" They knew before; now they know at a different level. "Knowing" is not just about ideas; it's about the engagement of the whole person: mind, senses, emotions, spirit, body, relationships. The more fully a person is engaged in what he or she is trying to know, the more fully that person will be able to respond to what is known, and the more energy he or she will be able to invest in what has to be done with that knowledge.

We have to engage abortion in all its dimensions in order to abolish it and do so fully. It was full engagement in what they were fighting that enabled Basil, Wilberforce, and Dr. King to accomplish what they achieved. So it will be with us. That full engagement is another way of saying *love*. The word, of course, is the most misused, abused, and confused word in the English language. I often heard Fulton Sheen point out that we use it with such divergent meanings: I love ice cream; I love my dog; I love my mother; I love God. And the word is used to justify some pretty evil things, like adultery, euthanasia, and abortion.

A wise man was once asked, "If you had the power to do anything at all, what would you do?" He replied, "I would restore words to their original meaning." Where do we find the original meaning of the word *love*? Scripture tells us, "This is how we know what love is. Jesus Christ laid down His life for us. And we ought to lay down our lives for our brothers" (1 John 3:16 NIV).

In other words, love is found on Calvary. Love's best symbol is not the heart but the cross. And the second lesson from this line of Scripture is that what Christ revealed to the world through the cross about the meaning of love, we must also reveal through our own sacrifice for those we love. That is why I have stressed in this book that we must give ourselves away in love, and be ready to sacrifice everything, for the unborn. The world can and must hear us speak up for the unborn, but they must also see us do things that make them scratch their heads and ask, "Why are these people sacrificing so much for them?"

This was one of the dynamics that led Dr. Bernard Nathanson, who had cofounded the abortion industry, to embrace the faith. He saw pro-life people sacrificing themselves, their reputations, their possessions, their freedom as they rescued the unborn, and he had to ask himself what made these people do this, what was the invisible force that impelled them. It helped him discover love, which in turn led him to faith.

Abortion is the exact opposite of love. Love says, "I sacrifice myself for the good of the other person." Abortion says, "I sacrifice the other person for the good of myself." And isn't it amazing that the very same words used by the culture of death to justify abortion are the words used by our Lord to proclaim life and salvation and love: *"This is My body!"*

"This is my body," some say. "I will do what I want, even if it means destroying the child." "This is My body," Jesus said, "given for you." (See Luke 22.) He did not cling to His body so that we would die but rather gave it away so that we could live. These are the words that define our mission in the world: spouse saying to spouse, parents saying to children, clergy saying to their congregations, all of us saying to our brothers and sisters, *"This is my body, my time, my efforts, my resources, my life—given for you, that you may live!"*

THE RIGHT TO LIFE

The line of thought I have traced in this book is simple and yet multifaceted. Human beings were created by God and belong to Him, and He calls them to organize themselves politically so they can secure the rights He gave them—starting with life. One of the greatest experiments of such political organizing came about in the United States of America, a nation uniting people not based on geography or ethnicity but on the principles of God-given rights. Our Founders did not only write about those principles but they also sacrificed for them. Abortion directly and thoroughly undermines those principles, and therefore its legalization constitutes the disintegration of the state itself. We are left, then, with the inescapable conclusion that we too are to pledge our lives, our fortunes, and our sacred honor to eradicate abortion.

The pro-life movement is not just about "promoting life." It is about restoring *the right to life* to those deprived of that fundamental right. It is a movement with a specific and targeted goal, namely, to see to it that human children, during their time in the womb, are recognized and protected as persons under the law, just as children and adults outside the womb are protected. The protection of the right to life has always been, is now, and always will be *the fundamental issue* for any society, nation, or Church. If that right is not secure, all our other efforts at building a world of justice, love, and peace are building on quicksand.

At the time of this writing, there is a furor over recent comments of Pope Francis that led some to believe he was asking people to focus less on the problem of abortion.[1] He was doing no such thing, but rather pointing out the connections between this issue and the very basis of the Gospel. But the more fundamental response to that concern—a response that would be valid even if the pope *were* trying to downplay the abortion issue—is that the urgent priority of defending the right to life doesn't come from the pope any more than the right itself does! It comes from our very humanity and from the God who created it. And the pope would be the first to acknowledge that he can't change that!

That's the overarching point of this book. Given that imperative, I have posed and begun to answer the next logical question, namely, what must we do next to break the stalemate and abolish abortion? Answering that question involves examining the duties as well as the failures of both church and state. Both of these entities have a fundamental duty to human rights and to the God who gave them. Neither has the authority to deny, veto, or edit human rights, or to deny, veto, or edit the human imperative to defend those rights.

You and I do not defend life because a president or pope tells us to, and we do not cease to be obliged to defend life if a president or pope tells us not to. This duty does not come from any authority of the Church or the state. Yet both church and state have become infected by "the great disconnect" that I have documented briefly in these pages. The unborn child, though we know more about her now than at any time in human history, has become the invisible member of the human family, the outcast who is both forgotten and insulted in ways that offend reason and common sense. So strong and pervasive is the prejudice against these children and the rejection of their claim to any recognition or protection that this prejudice and rejection quickly extend to all of us who speak up for and defend them. And therefore we have no choice but to accept and absorb that prejudice against us and that rejection of us in order to restore it for the children.

The time has come to rise up in solidarity with these children, which means, in and of itself, rising in solidarity with their moms and dads. Speaking for the children means that we reclaim for them the bond with their parents that is so essential to their own well-being! That is why our movement must, with equal force, show the reality of what abortion does to the child and to the mother and father. Social reform movements have not succeeded in the past without visualizing the victim, without confronting society with the pain and wounds that the victim experiences, all the while absolutely refusing to allow it to be hidden.

America will not reject abortion until America *sees* abortion. That is why we show images of abortion victims, and that is why we share testimonies of the moms and dads who are also victimized. The battle is concrete and specific, not abstract. It is not just about beliefs, but also about bloodshed. It is not just about viewpoints, but also about victims. It is not a matter of "agreeing to disagree" with the perpetrator of violence. It is a matter of stopping the perpetrator.

Our movement must increase the discomfort and tension that people experience by the fact that abortion continues. We do this by exposing abortion and the damage it does. We expose the procedure itself through descriptions, diagrams, photos, and videos. We expose the harm abortion does to moms and dads by sharing the testimonies they give of their pain and healing. We expose the corruption in the abortion industry, the malpractice and fraud, and the unscrupulous attitudes and actions of the abortion providers.

By reframing the conflict as one between a destructive abortion industry on the one hand and the family unit on the other, we help people overcome the ambivalence, confusion, and stalemate created when they can only understand this as a conflict between a mother and her child or between life and choice.

When the people of God intervene in the lives of these moms and dads by strengthening the efforts of pregnancy centers and sidewalk counselors and by closing abortion facilities, the numbers of abortions go down. When that happens, not only are lives being saved, but the abortion industry is also being weakened.

Judges and legislators will be more inclined to change public policy on abortion when they see that women are less inclined to seek it. They will be more inclined to declare abortion clinics illegal when they see fewer people using them. And public officials will be more willing to do their duty regarding the protection of the unborn the more they see a newly informed public clamor for it.

The Johnson Amendment must go because it simply has no basis in law, theology, or history. The government should not have one ounce of veto power over what is preached in a pulpit or taught by a church. On the way toward that goal, a bright-line test must be put into law so that churches and organizations that agree not to "intervene" in a political race know what that means. A simple identification of words and phrases that constitute an "endorsement" of a candidate would enable citizens to know where the line is that they are not supposed to cross before they act, rather than being scared into not acting at all because they "might" cross the line based on "all the facts and circumstances." And the institutional Church needs to stop hushing itself into silence and shackling the pro-life political efforts of the faithful because of these concerns.

HEED THE CRIES

The Church and the state have the ability to bring the legal abortion industry to an end. They simply lack the will. More specifically, they lack the will to make the necessary sacrifices to do so because too many people lack that moral and psychological imperative to do so, which springs from a full engagement with the reality of this tragedy and its victims. To the extent that the Church and the state are unwilling to fight the necessary fight, this tragedy will continue.

Abortion has undermined the very functioning of the state and the Church and has poisoned the system of both. When those who actively oppose abortion are under the authority of others who are still within that same poisoned structure, then those in authority will simply get rid of the troublemakers. They will suspend the public official, fire the broadcaster or businessperson, and sideline the pastor.

Someone once wrote, "The false god transforms suffering into violence; the true God transforms violence into suffering." Abortion kills thousands a day because the suffering of a pregnancy is transformed into the violence of child-killing. Abortion is stopped every day because some people are willing to absorb that violence and transform it, by the power of love, into personal suffering, which they accept for the sake of saving lives.

In the Old Testament, we read of child sacrifice, and I have mentioned in this book that Scripture indicates that the killing of children was the primary reason for the exile of both Israel and Judah. The people of God mingled with the nations around them, adopted their practices, and engaged in the worship of idols. This worship involved having children burned in the ovens contained in the statues of these idols. Some of the artwork depicting these practices shows priests beating on drums while the children are being sacrificed. Why the drums? The purpose was to drown out the cries of the children.

This is reminiscent, of course, of the story of the church near the tracks of the trains leading to concentration camps. People in the congregation complained to the pastor about the disturbing sound of people screaming in the trains when they passed during the Sunday worship service. "Tell them to sing a little louder" was the pastor's reply.[2] The beating of drums is all around us; the loud singing continues in our ears. We are told to pay attention to other issues, and not to be so aggressive or focused on this controversial issue. We are told, in a million ways, to accommodate ourselves to it.

And that is precisely the opposite of what we are to do. We are not to accommodate ourselves to child-killing. Rather, we are called to silence the drumbeat and the singing that is distracting us from hearing the victims' cries. We are to allow ourselves to hear those cries and allow our hearts to be broken and our souls to be disturbed and our eyes to fill with tears! Blessed are they who mourn! Ending abortion starts with a broken heart because only a heart that is broken can receive the grace to rise to the occasion and fight this great battle for life.

FROM VICTORY TO VICTORY

It is a battle we are winning, and will win, because we have already won! There is One among us who holds the keys of death and of hell. Jesus Christ is risen from the dead! By rising, He did not only destroy His death, but He also destroyed ours. He overcame the entire kingdom of death, robbing it of its power. Because of Christ's resurrection, death no longer has the final word in the human story. This means that the power of abortion—which takes more lives than any other evil—has also been broken. Our pro-life movement does not simply work for victory. We work from victory! Victory is our starting point. We joyfully proclaim to the world that Christ is risen, and that for this reason, we must choose life. We then work to apply that victory to every sector of society.

The labor is intense and the obstacles many. But we do not cower before the culture of death or scratch our heads and wonder how we will ever overcome it. Rather, we stand before it with victorious confidence and declare, "Be gone! You have no room here! No place here!

No further authority to menace the human family. Your kingdom has been conquered, and Christ reigns supreme!"

As we fight the battle, let us prepare for the victory celebration. We may come in limping because of the wounds we have absorbed along the way. But we will be there. Set up the tables. Keep the lights on. It won't be long. We will get to the Promised Land, together.

APPENDIX

The Beloved Community and the Unborn[1]

EVERY JANUARY OUR NATION PAUSES TO RECOMMIT ITSELF to fulfilling the dream of Martin Luther King Jr., and we reflect on how that dream touches every human life. Dr. King taught that justice and equality need to be as wide-reaching as humanity itself. Nobody can be excluded from the "Beloved Community." He taught that "injustice anywhere is a threat to justice everywhere."

In his 1967 Christmas sermon, he pointed out the foundation of this vision: "The next thing we must be concerned about if we are to have peace on earth and good will toward men is the nonviolent affirmation of the sacredness of all human life. . . . Man is a child of God, made in His image, and therefore must be respected as such. . . . And when we truly believe in the sacredness of human personality, we won't exploit people, we won't trample over people with the iron feet of oppression, we won't kill anybody."

Scripture teaches, "Seek first God's Kingdom and His righteousness and all else shall be yours as well" (Matt. 6:33). Dr. King humbled himself before God and became increasingly dependent on Him. Dr. King's search for the Beloved Community was really part of his search for the Kingdom of God. Because "God is Love" (1 John 4:16), His Kingdom is founded on love (*agape*). That is why, in his search for the Beloved Community, Dr. King discovered God's love.

The work of building the Beloved Community is far from finished. In each age, it calls us to fight against poverty, discrimination, and violence in every form. And as human history unfolds, the forms that discrimination and violence take will evolve and change. Yet our commitment to overcome them must not change, and we must not shrink from the work of justice, no matter how unpopular it may become.

In our day, therefore, we cannot ignore the discrimination, injustice, and violence that are being inflicted on the youngest and smallest members of the human family, the children in the womb. We must declare that these children too are members of the Beloved Community, that our destiny is linked with theirs, and that therefore they deserve justice, equality, and protection.

And we can pursue that goal, no matter what ethnic, religious, or political affiliation we have. None of that has to change in order for us to embrace Dr. King's affirmation of the sacredness of all human life. It simply means that in our efforts to set free the oppressed, we include the children in the womb.

We invite all people of goodwill to join us in the affirmation that children in the womb have equal rights and human dignity!

Dr. Alveda King, director, African-American Outreach, Priests for Life, niece of Martin Luther King Jr.

Fr. Frank Pavone, national director, Priests for Life

Mrs. Naomi Barber King, wife of the late Rev. A. D. King (brother of Martin Luther King Jr.)

Gloria Y. Jackson, Esq., great-granddaughter of Dr. Booker T. Washington, president, Booker T. Washington Inspirational Network

Rev. Derek King, pastor, Indianapolis, Indiana, nephew of Martin Luther King Jr.

Lynne M. Jackson, great-great-granddaughter of Dred Scott (and numerous other leaders)

ACKNOWLEDGMENTS

THE FUTURE PASSES BY WAY OF THE FAMILY, WHICH IS WHERE we first learn the things that are important to us. I want to express thanks, therefore, to my parents, Marion and Joe, and my brother, Joe. In particular I thank Mom and my grandmother Frances (whose maiden name was Vita, which means "Life") for taking me to my first March for Life in 1976. That event lit the spark of pro-life activism within me.

I can't imagine collaborators more loyal than Janet Morana, Anthony DeStefano, and Jerry Horn, who have accompanied me day by day in this pro-life battle and who provide so much personal and professional support, including in the writing of this book.

I'd especially like to thank the whole team at Thomas Nelson, my editors, Webster Younce and Katherine Rowley, as well as my literary manager, Peter Miller.

So many fanned those flames, from which this book takes its origin. In particular I am grateful for the encouragement that three popes have expressed to me personally for my work: Pope Saint John Paul II, Pope Benedict XVI, and Pope Francis. I am grateful to have known Bl. Mother Teresa of Calcutta, who taught me so much of what I have said in this book, and the same is true of my relationship with Cardinal John O'Connor, Father Benedict Groeschel, CFR, and Mother Angelica of EWTN. So many other Church leaders have helped me pave the way for this book, including Cardinal Renato Martino, Cardinal Christoph Schönborn, Archbishop Vincenzo Pagia, Archbishop Rino Fisichella, Bishop Ignacio Carrasco de Paula, and Bishop Michael Sheridan.

All my collaborators and staff at Priests for Life have provided immense help. It is a joy to work with our Pastoral Associates, including Fr. Denis G. Wilde, O.S.A., Fr. Walter Quinn, O.S.A., Fr. Victor Salomon, Msgr. Mike Mannion, Dr. Theresa Burke, Kevin Burke, Bryan Kemper, and Marie Smith. Thanks too to our pastoral associate Alveda King and her mom, Naomi, who provide a great witness that has helped shape this book. I am grateful for the research assistance of Geoffrey Strickland, Christa Childs, Anthony Vento and Leslie Palma, and the overall help of Mark Valonzo. I thank our civil attorneys, Robert Muise and David Yerushalmi, the American Freedom Law Center, and our Canonical advisor, Rev. David Deibel.

All my colleagues in pro-life leadership are a constant source of encouragement, and I always learn from them. For this book in particular, I want to thank Mark Crutcher, Troy Newman, Gregg Cunningham, the leadership of National Right to Life (especially David O'Steen, Darla St. Martin, and Ernie Ohlhoff), and Georgette Forney (who with Janet Morana cofounded the Silent No More Awareness Campaign).

A special acknowledgment is due to James Bopp Jr., whose expert leadership in the area of tax law has guided, inspired, and protected my work over many years. Thanks too to his associate Barry Bostrom.

Many others gave me input for this book, directly or indirectly, including my friends at Alliance Defending Freedom (especially Alan

Sears, Erik Stanley, and Matt Bowman), Deacon Keith Fournier, Dr. Deal Hudson, Russell Shaw, David Barton, Colin Hanna, Rev. John Ensor, Jay Sekulow, Joe Brinck, Tony Maas, Bernard Dobranski, William Brennan, Charles Watkins, and Gerard Bradley.

Particularly in the political arena, being in the trenches over the years with great men and women has helped form my vision for this book, and among many others, I'm grateful to Gov. Sam Brownback, Sen. Rick Santorum, Rep. Chris Smith, Ken Cucinelli (former attorney general of Virginia), Richard Viguerie, Ann Corkery, Mike Hernon, Martin Gillespie, Billy Valentine, and Marjorie Dannenfelser.

To so many priests and pastors who continue to courageously preach the Gospel of Life, and to so many lay persons of all denominations who exemplify the kind of commitment and sacrifice I call for in this book, I say thank you as well.

NOTES

INTRODUCTION: US AND THEM

1. "Whatsoever You Do . . .": Speech of Mother Teresa of Calcutta to the National Prayer Breakfast, Washington, DC, February 3, 1994 (transcript), http://www.priestsforlife.org/brochures/mtspeech.html.

ONE: IN THE PUBLIC SQUARE

1. Kathryn Jean Lopez, "Pro-Life? Not Welcome in Andrew Cuomo's New York," *National Review Online*, January 17, 2014, http://www.nationalreview.com/corner/368809/pro-life-not-welcome-andrew-cuomos-new-york-kathryn-jean-lopez.

2. Scott J. Hammond, Kevin R. Hardwick, and Howard L. Lubert, eds., *Classics of American Political and Constitutional Thought*, 2 vols. (Indianapolis: Hackett, 2007), 974.

3. *Boletín Eclesiástico de Filipínas: The Philippine Ecclesiastical Review* 82, nos. 855–57 (2006): 758.

4. Harden v. State, 216 S.W. 2d 708 (1949), http://web.novalis.org/cases/Harden%20v.%20State.html.

5. Hill v. State, 88 So. 2d 887 (1956).

6. Reynolds v. US, 98 U.S.145 (1878).

7. Suzanne T. Poppema, with Mike Henderson, *Why I Am an Abortion Doctor* (New York: Prometheus, 1996), 120.

8. Brenda Peterson, "Sister Against Sister," *New Age Journal*, September /October 1993, http://www.holysmoke.org/sdhok/abo015.htm.

9. Ginette Paris, *The Sacrament of Abortion* (Spring Publications, 1992).

10. M. Stanton Evans, *The Theme Is Freedom: Religion, Politics, and the American Tradition* (Washington, DC: Regnery, 1994), 82.

11. Ibid., 141.

12. Ibid., 121.

TWO: THE WORLD OF *ROE*

1. Roe v. Wade, 410 U.S. 113, 159 (1973).

2. Wade, 113 at 158.

3. John Paul II, *Veritatis Splendor* ("The Splendor of Truth"), August 6, 1993, par. 99, http://www.vatican.va/holy_father/john_paul_ii /encyclicals/documents/hf_jp-ii_enc_06081993_veritatis-splendor _en.html.

4. John Paul II, *The Gospel of Life (Evangelium Vitae)* (Pauline Books & Media, 1995), no. 20.

5. Nobel Lecture, December 11, 1979 (short excerpt), http://www .nobelprize.org/nobel_prizes/peace/laureates/1979/teresa -lecture.html.

6. "Whatsoever You Do . . .": Speech of Mother Teresa of Calcutta to the National Prayer Breakfast, Washington, DC, February 3, 1994 (transcript), http://www.priestsforlife.org/brochures/mtspeech.html.

7. Martin Rhonheimer and Paolo G. Carozza, "Fundamental Rights, Moral Law, and the Legal Defense of Life in a Constitutional Democracy: A Constitutionalist Approach to the Encyclical *Evangelium Vitae*," *American Journal of Jurisprudence* (1998): 153, 161.

8. George Weigel, *Evangelical Catholicism: Deep Reform in the 21st Century Church* (New York: Basic Books, 2013), 220–21.

9. US Catholic Bishops, *Living the Gospel of Life: A Challenge to American Catholics*, 1998, no. 4, http://www.usccb.org/issues-and -action/human-life-and-dignity/abortion/living-the-gospel-of-life.cfm.

10. Apostolic Journey to the United States of America and Canada: Farewell Ceremony: Address of His Holiness John Paul II, September 19, 1987, http://www.vatican.va/holy_father/john_paul_ii/speeches /1987/september/documents/hf_jp-ii_spe_19870919_congedo-stati -uniti_en.html.

11. Apostolic Journey to the United States of America and Canada: Farewell Ceremony: Address of His Holiness John Paul II, October 8, 1995, http://www.vatican.va/holy_father/john_paul_ii/speeches/1995/october/documents/hf_jp-ii_spe_19951008_congedo-usa_en.html.

12. Charter of the United Nations, preamble, available online from the Human Rights Library of the University of Minnesota, at http://www1.umn.edu/humanrts/instree/preamble.html.

13. "The Universal Declaration of Human Rights," preamble, http://www.un.org/en/documents/udhr/.

14. The United Nations International Covenant on Civil and Political Rights, part 3, art. 26, http://www.hrweb.org/legal/cpr.html.

15. See Declaration of the Rights of the Child, online at UNICEF's page, http://www.unicef.org/lac/spbarbados/Legal/global/General/declaration_child1959.pdf; and Convention on the Rights of the Child, at the website of the Office of the High Commissioner of Human Rights, at http://www.ohchr.org/EN/ProfessionalInterest/Pages/CRC.aspx.

THREE: TIME FOR REPENTANCE

1. Elie Wiesel, Nobel Peace Prize acceptance speech, December 10, 1986, http://www.nobelprize.org/nobel_prizes/peace/laureates/1986/wiesel-acceptance_en.html.

2. "Senator Obama's Inhuman Voting Record on Infanticide," transcript of *The Rush Limbaugh Show*, August 18, 2008, http://www.rushlimbaugh.com/daily/2008/08/18/senator_obama_s_inhuman_voting_record_on_infanticide.

3. Roe v. Wade, 410 U.S. 113, 158 (1973).

4. John Ensor, *Innocent Blood: Challenging the Powers of Death with the Gospel of Life* (Adelphi, MD: Cruciform Press, 2011), 84.

5. Ibid., 72.

6. Adapted from Tertullian, *The Apology*, trans. S. Thelwall, chap. 39, http://www.logoslibrary.org/tertullian/apology/39.html.

FOUR: THE IRREPRESSIBLE SPIRITUAL IMPERATIVE

1. George Grant, *Third Time Around: A History of the Pro-life Movement from the First Century to the Present* (Brentwood, TN: Wolgemuth & Hyatt, 1991), 20–21.

2. William Wilberforce, "Abolition Speech" to Parliament on May 12, 1789, http://www.artofmanliness.com/abolition-speech-by-william-wilberforce/.

3. Eric Metaxas, *Amazing Grace: William Wilberforce and the Heroic Campaign to End Slavery* (New York: HarperOne, 2007), 159.

4. Ibid., 163.

5. Martin Luther King Jr., "Letter from a Birmingham Jail," April 16, 1963, available online from Bates College, at http://abacus.bates.edu /admin/offices/dos/mlk/letter.html.

6. "Congresswoman Rosa L. DeLauro Press Release," February 28, 2006, Priests for Life, http://www.priestsforlife.org/pressreleases /statementprinciples.htm.

7. George Orwell, *Nineteen Eighty-Four* (London: Martin Secker & Warburg, 1949), pt. 1, chap. 3, 32.

8. Keith Ablow, "Who Would Kill Children?" Fox News, Opinion, December 14, 2012, http://www.foxnews.com/opinion/2012/12/14 /who-would-kill-children/.

9. "Melissa Harris-Perry: Verdict Means It's OK to Kill Innocent Black Children," Breitbart, July 13, 2013, http://www.breitbart.com /Breitbart-TV/2013/07/13/Melissa-Harris-Perry-this-verdict-means -its-ok-to-kill-innocent-black-children.

10. "Obama's Commencement Address at Notre Dame" (transcript), *New York Times*, May 17, 2009, http://www.nytimes.com/2009/05/17/us /politics/17text-obama.html?pagewanted=all&_r=1&.

11. John Ensor, *Innocent Blood: Challenging the Powers of Death with the Gospel of Life* (Adelphi, MD: Cruciform Press, 2011), 13.

12. John Paul II, *The Gospel of Life (Evangelium Vitae)* (Pauline Books & Media, 1995), no. 9.

FIVE: FREEDOM OF SPEECH

1. New York Times Co. v. Sullivan, 376 U.S. 254, 270 (1964).

2. Citizens United v. Federal Election Commission, 558 U.S. 310 (2010).

3. Branch Ministries v. Rossotti, 211 F.3d 137 (D.C. Cir. 2000).

4. Erik W. Stanley, "LBJ, the IRS, and Churches: The Unconstitutionality of the Johnson Amendment in Light of Recent Supreme Court Precedent," *Regent University Law Review* 24, no. 2 (2011–2012): 241; online at http://www.speakupmovement.org/Church/Content/PDF /01Stanleyvol.24.2.pdf.

5. Ibid., 243.
6. "Charities, Churches and Politics," IRS website, upd. July 12, 2007, http://www.irs.gov/uac/Charities,-Churches-and-Politics.
7. Stanley, "LBJ, the IRS, and Churches," 247.
8. Ibid., 248.
9. Ibid., 249.
10. Ibid.
11. Ibid., 250–51.
12. United States Conference of Catholic Bishops, *Political Activity Guidelines for Catholic Organizations*, July 2014, http://www.usccb.org/about/general-counsel/political-activity-guidelines.cfm.
13. Stanley, "LBJ, the IRS, and Churches," 252.
14. Grayned v. City of Rockford, 408 U.S. 104 (1972); see https://supreme.justia.com/cases/federal/us/408/104/case.html.
15. Virginia v. Hicks, 539 U.S. 113, 119 (2003); see http://law2.umkc.edu/faculty/projects/ftrials/conlaw/virginiavhicks.html.
16. Stanley, "LBJ, the IRS, and Churches," 255.
17. Rossotti at 142–43.
18. Sullivan at 270.
19. Buckley v. Valeo, 424 U.S. (1976).
20. Rev. Rul. 2004–6, § 527(e)(2); http://www.irs.gov/pub/irs-drop/rr-04-6.pdf, p. 4.
21. *Bopp, Coleson & Bostro*m (Terre Haute, IN), Letter to K. Krawczyk, Internal Reveue Service, on behalf of Priests for Life, January 27, 2005.

SIX: FREEDOM OF THE PULPIT

1. Congressman Walter Jones, Congressional Record-House, September 12, 2002, 16656.
2. Citizens United v. Federal Election Commission, 558 U.S. ___ (2010); https://supreme.justia.com/cases/federal/us/558/08–205/opinion.html.
3. Hosanna-Tabor Evangelical Lutheran Church & School v. EEOC, 565 U.S. ____ (2012); http://www.supremecourt.gov/opinions/11pdf/10–553.pdf, 15.
4. Internal Revenue Service, *Tax Guide for Churches and Organizations*, http://www.irs.gov/pub/irs-pdf/p1828.pdf, 12.

5. Ibid., 7.

6. Second Vatican Council, *Pastoral Constitution on the Church in the Modern World* (*Gaudium et Spes*), no. 76, http://www.vatican.va/archive /hist_councils/ii_vatican_council/documents/vat-ii_cons_19651207 _gaudium-et-spes_en.html.

7. US Catholic Bishops, *Living the Gospel of Life: A Challenge to American Catholics*, 1998, no. 33, http://www.usccb.org/issues-and -action/human-life-and-dignity/abortion/living-the-gospel-of-life.cfm.

SEVEN: PROOF OF PASSIVITY

1. Buckley v. Valeo, 424 U.S. (1976), emphasis added.

2. United States Conference of Catholic Bishops, "Pastoral Plan for Pro-Life Activities: A Campaign in Support of Life," http://www.usccb.org /about/pro-life-activities/pastoral-plan-prolife-activities.cfm, accessed September 10, 2014.

3. Fr. Steve Lantry, S.J., Letter to parishioners of St. Leo Church, Tacoma, WA, October 28, 2004.

4. John Ensor, *Innocent Blood: Challenging the Powers of Death with the Gospel of Life* (Adelphi, MD: Cruciform Press, 2011), 72.

EIGHT: OPEN WINDOWS

1. *Bopp, Coleson & Bostrom* (Terre Haute, IN), Letter to Priests for Life, February 23, 2004.

2. Russell Shaw, *Nothing to Hide: Secrecy, Communication, and Communion in the Catholic Church* (San Francisco: Ignatius, 2008), 163–64, quoting John Paul II, apostolic letter *Novo Millennio Ineunte* (At the Beginning of the New Millennium), January 6, 2001, no. 45.

3. Ibid., 62, quoting from the Second Vatican Council, *Dogmatic Constitution on the Church (Lumen Gentium)*, no. 32.

4. Shaw, *Nothing to Hide*, 15.

5. Ibid., 63, quoting Pope Paul VI, encyclical *Ecclesiam Suam*, 115–16.

6. Ibid., 99, quoting *Lumen Gentium*, 37.

7. Ibid., 124, quoting Germain Grisez.

8. Second Vatican Council, *Pastoral Constitution on the Church in the Modern World* (*Gaudium et Spes*), no. 92, http://www.vatican .va/archive/hist_councils/ii_vatican_council/documents/vat-ii_cons _19651207_gaudium-et-spes_en.html.

9. Bernard V. Brady, *Essential Catholic Social Thought* (Maryknoll, NY: Orbis, 2008), 175.

10. Robert Moynihan, "Letter #82: The Peacemaker," *The Moynihan Letters*, August 31, 2013, http://themoynihanletters.com/from-the-desk-of/letter-82-the-peacemaker.

NINE: COLLISION COURSE

1. Justice O'Connor, with whom Justices White and Rehnquist join, dissenting, in Akron v. Akron Center for Reproductive Health, 462 U.S. 416, at 456–58.

2. R. Seth Williams, *Investigation of the Women's Medical Society in Philadelphia: Report of the Grand Jury* (Darby, PA: Diane, 2011), 13.

3. Peter Singer and Helga Kuhse, "On Letting Handicapped Infants Die," in *The Right Thing to Do*, James Rachels, editor (New York: Random House, 1989), 146.

4. Peter Singer, *Rethinking Life and Death: The Collapse of Our Traditional Ethics*, repr. ed. (New York: St. Martin's Griffin, 1996), 210.

5. John McCormack, "Video: Planned Parenthood Official Argues for Right to Post-Birth Abortion," *The Blog* (by *Weekly Standard*), March 29, 2013, Weeklystandard.com/blogs/video-planned-parenthood -official-argues-right-post-birth-abortion_712198.html.

6. Alberto Giubilini and Francesca Minerva, "After-Birth Abortion: Why Should the Baby Live?" *Journal of Medical Ethics* (2011), http://jme.bmj.com/content/early/2012/03/01/medethics-2011–100411.full.

7. See Craig R. Ducat, *Constitutional Interpretation: Rights of the Individual*, vol. 2, 10th ed. (New York: Cengage Learning, 2012), 769.

8. Planned Parenthood v. Rounds, 686 F.3d 889 (8th Cir. 2012).

9. National Abortion Federation, et. al. v. Ashcroft, 330 F. Supp. 2d 436 (S.D.N.Y. 2004); transcript highlights available from the American Center for Law and Justice, at http://media.aclj.org/pdf/nyhighlightspbadoc.pdf.

10. Gonzales v. Carhart, 550 U.S. 124 (2007); syllabus available online from Cornell University's Legal Information Institute, at http://www.law.cornell.edu/supct/html/05–380.ZS.html.

11. Frank Pavone, Open Letter to Nancy Pelosi, posted on the website of Priests for Life, June 18, 2013, http://www.priestsforlife.org/pelosi/.

12. Steven Ertelt, "Pelosi Ridicules Letter Asking Her to Condemn Abortion or Renounce Catholicism," LifeNews.com, June 25, 2013, http://www.lifenews.com/2013/06/25/pelosi-ridicules-letter-asking -her-to-condemn-abortion-or-renounce-catholicism/.

13. Steven Ertelt, "Priest Says Pelosi Has Admitted Her Abortion Position Is Not Catholic," LifeNews.com, June 26, 2013, http://www.lifenews. com/2013/06/26/priest-says-pelosi-has-admitted-her-abortion -position-is-not-catholic/.

14. See www.PriestsForLife.org/IsThisWhatYouMean.

15. *USA Today*/Gallup poll, December 27–30, 2012, http://www. pollingreport.com/abortion.htm.

16. FOX News documentary *See No Evil-The Kermit Gosnell Case*, aired May 3, 2013. To obtain a copy of this documentary, visit www. FoxNews.com/Specials.

17. See the text and caricature at the Royal Museums Greenwich's *The Abolition of the Slave Trade* page, at http://collections.rmg.co.uk /collections/objects/128067.html.

18. See Christopher Metress, *The Lynching of Emmett Till: a Documentary Narrative (The American South)* (New York: Univ. of Virginia Press, 2002), 16.

19. Martin Luther King Jr., "Letter from a Birmingham Jail," April 16, 1963, available online from Bates College, at http://abacus.bates.edu /admin/offices/dos/mlk/letter.html.

20. Michelle Bogre, *Photography as Activism: Images for Social Change* (New York: Focal Press, 2011), 34.

21. http://digitalassets.ushmm.org/photoarchives/detail. aspx?id=1045556.

22. Reuters, "Lawmaker Criticizes 'Schindler's List' Airing Wednesday, February 26, 1997," http://www.writing.upenn.edu/~afilreis/Holocaust /schindler-on-tv.html; accessed September 11, 2014.

23. Douglas P. Shuit, "Grisly Photos Give Students Reality Check: Schools: Two doctors give a slide show depicting injuries from gunshots and stabbings. It is designed to strip romance from violence and counter TV images," *Los Angeles Times*, July 8, 1995, http:// articles.latimes.com/1995–07–08/local/me-21553_1_slide-show.

24. Linda Deutsch, "Judge Allows Prosecution Evidence; Defense Might Call Sydney Simpson," AP News Archive, July 7, 1995, http://www.

apnewsarchive.com/1995/Judge-Allows-Prosecution-Evidence
-Defense-Might-Call-Sydney-Simpson/id-b5f6c04c9fb7cf6b5712525f
d30e231d.

25. "Graphic Photos Work!" Priests for Life, Education Resources page,
accessed September 11, 2014, http://www.priestsforlife.org/brochures
/graphic-photos-work.htm.

26. Ibid.

27. View *Harder Truth* at www.youtube.com/abortionNOorg.

28. John Paul II, *The Gospel of Life (Evangelium Vitae)* (Pauline Books &
Media, 1995), no. 58.

29. Theresa Burke and J. Kevin Burke, "Let's Talk About Graphic
Pictures," on the Priests for Life page Looking Abortion in the Eye,
accessed September 11, 2014, http://www.priestsforlife.org/images
/post-abortion-healing.htm.

30. Gary S. Berger, William E. Brenner, and Louis G. Keith, eds., *Second
Trimester Abortion: Perspectives After a Decade of Experience*
(Hague, NETH: Martinus Nijhoff, 1981), 242, 245.

TEN: MOTHER AND CHILD

1. See http://www.lifesitenews.com/news/actress-jennifer-oneill-
announces-she-will-join-west-coast-walk-for-life.

2. Zel Miller, *A National Party No More* (Atlanta: Stroud & Hall, 2003),
106.

3. Jordan Strauss/WireImage, "Kourtney Kardashian Agonized
over Whether to Keep Her Baby," *People*, August 19, 2009, http://
celebritybabies.people.com/2009/08/19/kourtney-kardashian
-agonized-over-whether-to-keep-her-baby/.

4. Gonzales v. Carhart, 550 U.S. (2007), at 159.

5. James Davis and Tom Smith, 2013, General Social Surveys 1972–2013
(data file). Available at http://www.norc.uchicago.edu/GSS+Website
/Download.

6. Tamar Lewin, "Rape and Incest: Just 1% of All Abortions," *New York
Times*, October 13, 1989, http://www.nytimes.com/1989/10/13/us
/rape-and-incest-just-1-of-all-abortions.html.

7. George Skelton, "The Times Poll: Most Americans Think Abortion Is
Immoral," *Los Angeles Times*, March 19, 1989, http://articles.latimes.
com/1989–03–19/news/mn-450_1_oppose-abortion.

8. The Free Library, s.v. "25 Years of Abortion Polls: Support for Pro-Life Policies and Legislation Growing," accessed September 11, 2014 from http://www.thefreelibrary.com/25+Years+of+Abortion+Polls%3a+Support+for+Pro-Life+Policies+and . . . -a055342463; Carey Goldberg with Janet Elder, "Public Still Backs Abortion, But Wants Limits, Poll Says," *New York Times* Archives, January 16, 1998, http://www.nytimes.com/1998/01/16/us/public-still-backs-abortion-but-wants-limits-poll-says.html.

9. Pope John Paul II, *Crossing the Threshold of Hope* (New York: Random House Large Print in association with Alfred A. Knopf, 1995), 197–98.

10. John Paul II, *The Gospel of Life (Evangelium Vitae)* (Pauline Books & Media, 1995), no. 99.

11. Philip Ney, "Abortion, Conscience Clauses, and the Practice of Medicine," LifeNews.com, December 2, 2010, http://www.lifenews.com/2010/12/02/opi-1025/.

12. Janet Morana, *Recall Abortion: Ending the Abortion Industry's Exploitation of Women* (Charlotte: Saint Benedict Press, 2013).

13. See www.MissionariesoftheGospelofLife.com.

ELEVEN: A FOUNDATION OF LOVE

1. See http://www.nytimes.com/2013/09/20/world/europe/pope-bluntly-faults-churchs-focus-on-gays-and-abortion.html?pagewanted=all&_r=0.

2. See http://www.SingLouderMovie.com.

APPENDIX

1. Originally published at http://www.priestsforlife.org/africanamerican/beloved-community-and-the-unborn.htm.

ABOUT THE AUTHOR

FR. FRANK PAVONE IS ONE OF THE MOST PROMINENT PRO-LIFE leaders in the world. Born in Port Chester, New York, in 1959, he was ordained in 1988 for the Archdiocese of New York by Cardinal John O'Connor. In 1993, he became national director of Priests for Life and since then has served full-time in pro-life leadership with his bishop's permission. In 2005, he became a priest of the Diocese of Amarillo, Texas, at the invitation of Bishop John Yanta, who wanted to establish a Priests for Life presence there.

Fr. Frank is also the president of the National Pro-life Religious Council, an organization that unites leaders from many different denominations. He is the national pastoral director of the Silent No More Awareness Campaign and of Rachel's Vineyard, the world's largest ministry of healing after abortion.

He travels throughout the country to an average of four states every week, preaching and teaching against abortion. He produces programs regularly for religious and secular radio and television networks. He was asked by Mother Teresa to speak in India on the life issues and has addressed the pro-life caucus of the United States House of Representatives.

The Vatican appointed Fr. Frank to the Pontifical Council for the Family, which coordinates the pro-life activities of the Catholic Church. He also serves as a member of the Vatican's Pontifical Academy for Life. He was present at the bedside of Terri Schiavo as she was dying and was an outspoken advocate for her life. He was invited by members of the Class of 2009 at Notre Dame to lead an alternate commencement ceremony for those students who refused to attend the ceremony in which President Obama was honored. Fr. Frank was invited by members of Congress to preach at the prayer service they had in the Capitol just prior to the vote on health care reform. He received the Proudly Pro-life Award by the National Right to Life Committee, and numerous other pro-life awards and honorary doctorates. Norma McCorvey, the "Jane Roe" of the Supreme Court's *Roe vs. Wade* abortion decision, called Fr. Frank "the catalyst that brought me into the Catholic Church."

Fr. Frank is the author of two other books, *Ending Abortion, Not Just Fighting It* and *Pro-life Reflections for Every Day.*